EDUCATION IN THE AGE OF TRANSFORMATION

Emerging Directions and Future Strategies

ABOUT THE EDITORS

Dr. Samiran Kalita is currently serving as an Assistant Professor in Department of Education at Dhing College, Dhing, Nagaon. He holds his Doctoral Degree in Education from Rajiv Gandhi University (A Central University), Arunachal Pradesh. His research interests lie in the fields of Educational Psychology, Sociology of Education and Human psychology. He has numerous publications to his credit which comprises several research papers and book chapters in the field of education and psychology. Apart from presenting a number of insightful papers at various national and international seminars, he has obtained his M.Phil. Degree from Mizoram University (A Central University), Aizawl and completed his U.G. P.G. from Gauhati University, Guwahati.

Dr. Nandita Chitrakar is presently working as an Assistant Professor in the Department of Education at Girijananda Chowdhury University, where she is actively involved in both academic instruction and scholarly research. She has successfully cleared National level Eligibility Test (UGC-NET), State Level Eligibility Test (SLET). Dr. Chitrakar earned her Ph.D. in Education from Rajiv Gandhi University (A Central University). She completed both her Master's degree in Education and Bachelor of Education (B.Ed.) from Tezpur University. In addition, she holds a Post Graduate Diploma in Educational Management and Administration from IGNOU, enhancing her knowledge in institutional leadership and educational administration. Dr. Chitrakar has published a number of research papers and book chapters and has presented her work at various national and international seminars and conferences. Her primary area of interest is Educational Psychology, where she continues to explore the psychological principles that shape effective teaching and learning.

Dr. Nisanth. P.M. holds M.Sc. in Psychology, M.Ed., and a Ph.D. in Education from Pondicherry University (A Central University) in Puducherry. He has qualified the UGC NET-JRF in Education and he has supervised four doctoral thesis. He has been serving as Assistant Professor in the Department of Education at Rajiv Gandhi University (A Central University), Arunachal Pradesh, for the past nine years. His academic interests and areas of specialisation include Educational Psychology, Gender and Education, and the application of Artificial Intelligence in Education.

EDUCATION IN THE AGE OF TRANSFORMATION

Emerging Directions and Future Strategies

Dr. Samiran Kalita

Dr. Nandita Chitrakar

Dr. Nisanth. P. M.

ACADEMIC ENCLAVE

First Edition, 2026

ISBN: 978-93-48642-64-6 (Hardback)

Printed at Replika Press Pvt. Ltd.

Published by

ACADEMIC ENCLAVE™

House No. 10/15, Ground Floor,
Block-A, Street No. 14/3, Kamal Vihar,
Kamal Pur, Burari, Delhi-110084

Email: info@academicenclave.com

Mobile/Phone: +91-7042423166, 011-45502728

Website: www.academicenclave.com

Preface

Education across the world is undergoing an unprecedented phase of transformation. Rapid technological innovations, changing learner needs, and evolving societal expectations are reshaping how education is understood and practiced. The book "Education in the Age of Transformation: Emerging Directions and Future Strategies" brings together diverse perspectives from academicians, scholars, researchers, and practitioners on how education is adapting to these new realities. It explores critical themes such as Psychology, Well-being, and Learner Development, Pedagogical Approaches and the Role of Teachers, Technology and Innovation in Education, and Educational Transformations and Emerging Paradigms in the context of contemporary educational challenges.

Divided into four sections, the book begins with a discussion on psychology, well-being, and learner development, emphasizing the importance of mental health and emotional balance within educational settings. The second section highlights the evolving roles of teachers in today's classrooms, focusing on pedagogical approaches, resilience, and the teacher's role in fostering student well-being. The third section examines technology and innovation in education, presenting studies on artificial intelligence, virtual learning, and emerging teaching strategies that redefine the learning experience. The final section reflects on educational reforms, governance, and the paradigm shifts required to meet the challenges of the 21st century.

This edited volume serves as a timely contribution to ongoing academic dialogue, aiming to inspire educators, policymakers, and researchers to envision a more inclusive, adaptive, and future ready educational system. The chapters included here reflect not only scholarly rigor but also deep concern for the human side of education and its values, emotions, and transformative potential.

We express our heartfelt gratitude to all the contributing authors for their insightful thoughts and dedicated efforts in making this compilation possible. Their valuable contributions have enriched this book with diverse ideas and perspectives that truly reflect the spirit of transformation in education.

Editors

Contents

Section III: Technology and Innovation in Education

Section IV: Educational Transformations and Emerging Paradigms

Section I: Psychology, Well-being, and Learner Development

1

Positive Psychological Capital in Relation to Organizational Commitment and Quality of Work Life: A Comparative Analysis between Government and Private School Teachers of Arunachal Pradesh

Dr. Kakali Goswami* & Tapa Zingba**

**Assistant Professor & **MA Psychology IV Semester, Department of Psychology, Rajiv Gandhi University, Rono Hills, Doimukh, Arunachal Pradesh*

Email: kakali.goswami@rgu.ac.in

Abstract

The present study examined the relationship between psychological capital, organizational commitment and quality of work life among the tribal school teachers of Arunachal Pradesh. The dimensions of psychological capital included self-efficacy, hope, optimism and resilience and these are found to be correlated with productivity, performance at work and other behaviors at work in previous literature. The present study is a descriptive research applied correlational design to study the variables. The variables were measured quantitatively by administering standardized psychological tests namely Psychological capital questionnaire, Organizational commitment questionnaire and Work-Related Quality Of Life (WQRL) Scale. The data were collected from 200 tribal school teachers working in government and private run schools located in Arunachal Pradesh. The results were obtained by applying descriptive statistics, t test and Pearson correlation coefficient technique. The findings showed that only continuance commitment differ significantly between government and private teachers. The findings showed that psychological capital, affective and normative commitment differ significantly between male and female teachers of Arunachal Pradesh. The three dimensions of organizational commitment positively correlated psychological capital and it was significant. The finding also showed that psychological capital was positively correlated to quality of work life and it was significant. The study addressed the importance of positive psychological resources among school teachers for improve commitment and quality of work life.

Keywords: *Psychological capital, organizational commitment, quality of work life, school teacher, tribal school*

Introduction

An organization's success, and the capacity to actualize their goals, depends on the psychological resources and physical participation of human resources and effective management. The Psychological resources can be named as positive psychological Capital focuses on harnessing positive attitudes and feedback to enhance individual and group functioning. It encompasses measurable applications that contribute to performance increases in organizations. The four fundamental components of psychological capital are self-efficacy, hope, optimism, and resilience which are crucial for building a foundation of positive psychological well-being, fostering improved performance and sustainable growth. Fred Luthans developed this concept of psychological capital, which is based on the higher-order concept of positive organizational behaviour (POB). Positive effects of psychological capital on motivation, performance, and work satisfaction are seen in existing literature (Zhang et al., 2024; Jia & Zhang, 2024). Positive feelings and attitudes about work are associated with job satisfaction, which affects productivity and organizational commitment. Likewise, psychological capital elements like resilience, optimism, and self-efficacy are positively correlated with performance. Improved performance and higher-quality services are a result of motivation, which is fueled by elements like hope and self-efficacy. Employee productivity and retention depend heavily on organizational commitment which can be characterized as a person's identification and participation in an organization. Organizational commitment is essential for stability and effectiveness given the difficulty of keeping and inspiring workers in the twenty-first century. The key dimensions are emotional attachment, perceived obligation, and economic factors, respectively, which are reflected in affective, normative, and continuance commitment. In the workplace, organizational commitment refers to the connection workers have with their organization. In general, dedicated workers see a sense of belonging, a sense of connection with their organization, and a comprehension of the organization's objectives. These workers bring value since they are typically more committed to their task, exhibit comparatively high productivity, and take the initiative to offer assistance when needed. Affective commitment and normative commitment vary depending on the culture, with affective commitment being higher in individualistic societies and normative commitment being higher in collectivist cultures (Fischer and Mansell, 2009). Existing literature found that supervisor-related outcomes are predicted by commitment to the supervisor, but organizational-level outcomes are predicted by commitment to the organization (Wasti and Can, 2008). In a meta-analysis spanning 57 nations between 1984 and 2010 findings showed clear distinctions between collectivist and individualistic cultures in terms of affective, normative and continuance commitment (Meyer et al., 2012).

Psychological capital is well connected to quality of work life in an organization. Educational institutes are special organization committed for the nurturing of future generation of a country. The teachers are main workforce and they need to have a higher quality of work life to perform at best. A company's ability to draw in and keep skilled workers depends on its quality of work life which benefits both workers and employers. But there are less available literature in quality of work life of teachers at school level. Quality of work life refers to a range of workplace characteristics that support effective human resource development. The meaning of Quality of work life is shaped by personal perspectives, making it subjective. High-level employee engagement in decision-making is a feature of industrial democracy, but administrators' primary focus is on improving psychological elements of work to increase efficiency. Healthy working conditions, job security, and equitable profit sharing are top priorities when assessing quality of work life. There four basic principles of quality of work life (Herrick, H. Q., 1981).These are such as security principle, equity principle, individualism principle, democratic principle.

A relationship exists between Positive Psychological Capital, Organizational Commitment, and Quality of Work Life, which applies particularly in government and private schools teachers. Previous findings showed that higher level of Psychological capital that embodies hope, efficacy, resilience, and optimism relates favorably to organizational commitment by the teachers and also contributes positively to quality of work life. This relationship is important to consider when comparing public school teachers and private school teachers because the different work settings may have some impact on the said factors (Awaliah & Ingarianti, 2024; Perveen et al., 2025). Literature revealed that the efficacy and optimism have strong relationships with career commitment in teachers (Awaliah & Ingarianti, 2024). The quality of work life of private school teachers is much higher than their government school counterparts and 94% of private school teachers are on the high range(Sharma et al., 2023).This gap shows the possibility that the work environment of private schools is likely more supportive of higher quality of psychological resources and commitment.

Psychological capital, comprising hope, resilience, optimism, and self-efficacy, has been shown to enhance the quality of life among educators. For instance, a study in Kwara State, Nigeria, found a positive correlation between hope and resilience with quality of life among secondary school tutors (Olanrewaju & Tinuke, 2022).In rural settings of India the need for more research on psychological capital among teachers is emphasized, indicating a gap in understanding its specific effects in these communities(Clarence et al., 2021).Teachers in tribal areas may encounter distinct socio-economic and cultural barriers that influence their psychological capital and overall work life. Factors such as inadequate resources, bureaucratic pressures, and community engagement can significantly affect their psychological well-being (Çimen & Özgan, 2018).The impact of these challenges on psychological capital and quality of work life remains underexplored, suggesting a need for targeted studies. In contrast, while some research highlights the positive effects of psychological capital on job satisfaction and burnout among educators in different regions (Hansen et al., 2015), the specific context of tribal communities requires further investigation to understand the nuances of these relationships.

Methods and Materials

Sample

The study comprised of school level teachers of Arunachal Pradesh from both government and private school participated in this study. The sample of this study consist 200 school teachers (N=200, M=100, F=100), 100 from government school and 100 from private school. Furthermore out of 100 government school teachers, 50 were male and 50 were female similarly out of 100 private school teachers, 50 were male and 50 were female. The study included domicile of Arunachal Pradesh only

Measures

The study has measured the variables of the study by administering standardized psychological questionnaire were distributed to different regions of schools of Arunachal Pradesh both govt. and private school teachers with clear instruction by taking permission from their respective head of the school.

Psychological Capital Questionnaire (PCQ):

Psychological Capital Questionnaire scale was developed by Fred Luthans, Bruce J. Avolio& James B. Avey and consist of 24 items and 6-point likert scale (score as 1-6 from strongly disagree, Disagree, somewhat disagree, somewhat agree, agree and Strongly Agree). Four dimensions were present; a)Efficacy: items 1-6, b)Hope: items 7-12, Resilience: items 13-18, (13 is reverse scored) and Optimism: items 19-24 (20 and 23 are reverse scored).

Organizational Commitment Scale:

The test was created by Natalie J. Allen and John P. Meyer, is to evaluate an individual's degree of organizational commitment into three categories: affective, continuation, and normative commitment. It scale evaluates how committed workers are to their jobs, how much they identify with their company, and how likely they are to stick with them in the long run. The scale contains of 24 likert-type scale items, on which respondents indicate which statements about each aspect of job commitment they agree or disagree with. Higher ratings suggest greater levels of dedication to the position or company in that extent. There are nine negative and fifteen positive phrases on the scale. The following are the negative statements: 4, 5, 6, 8, 9, 12, 18, 19, and 24. The coefficient alpha, or dependability, for each scale was as follows: .87 for affective commitment,75 for continuity, and.79 for normative commitment. The likert-type seven-point for this test, the scoring system was kept at 1–7 (strongly disagree, disagree somewhat, disagree, uncertain, agree, slightly agree, strongly agree) for positive statements and 7–1 for negative items.

Work-Related Quality Of Life (WQRL) Scale:

The Work-related Quality of Life (WRQoL) scale is a tool used to evaluate different facets of employees' workplace quality of life. This scale was developed by Van Laar, D., Edwards, J. A., & Easton (2007). The scale includes several variables, such as job satisfaction, general life satisfaction, work-life balance, physical and psychological well-being, and work environment. Twenty-five questions make up the test: Six pieces each from JCS and GWB. Three questions each from HWI, CAW, and WCS, two questions from SAW, and one general question. The individual factor subscale and the overall WRQoL average both demonstrated test-retest validity, with r =.874** indicating a strong, substantial, positive intra-class correlation between the test and the retest measures. For this test, the five-point Likert-type scoring system was used. The elements with a negative value are items 7, 9, and 19.

Procedure

During the process of data collection, the researcher formed a good rapport and informed consent was taken from with participant. The study objectives were explained and ethical standards are followed. The data was collected by using survey method and informed consent.

Results:

Descriptive statistics

Table 4.1: Level of participants in all variables

Variables	*Groups*	*Mean*	*Status*
Psychological capital	Govt. school	109.18	Above moderate
	Private school	109.19	Above moderate
Affective commitment	Govt. school	38.87	Above moderate
	Private school	38.24	Above moderate
Normative commitment	Govt. school	35.78	Above moderate
	Private school	34.55	Above moderate
Continuance commitment	Govt. school	35.33	Above moderate
	Private school	37.33	Above moderate
Quality of Work Life	Govt. school	84.77	moderate
	Private school	83.64	moderate

The results showed that the level of Psychological capital is above moderate among government and private school teachers. It also showed that in all the three dimensions of organizational commitment is above moderate but the level of Quality of Work Life is moderate.

Inferential Statistics

Table 4.2: Mean, SD and t values result of variables between government and private teachers

Variables	*Groups*	*N*	*Mean*	*SD*	*t test*
Psychological capital	Govt. school	100	109.18	10.135	.007
	Private school	100	109.19	10.228	
Affective commitment	Govt. school	100	38.87	6.704	.622
	Private school	100	38.24	7.595	
Normative commitment	Govt. school	100	35.78	6.698	1.427
	Private school	100	34.55	5.426	
Continuance commitment	Govt. school	100	35.33	4.961	2.653**
	Private school	100	37.33	5.677	
Quality of Work Life	Govt. school	100	84.77	10.105	.687
	Private school	100	83.64	12.984	

*** p<.01 level*

The four independent sample t test was conducted to measure whether psychological capital, affective commitment, normative commitment, continuance commitment and quality of work life scores differ significantly between government and private school teachers. The result showed that there is significant difference in scores of government and private school teachers in terms of continuance commitment.

Table 4.3: Mean, SD and t-test result of variables between male and female teachers

Variables	*Groups*	*N*	*Mean*	*SD*	*t test*
Psychological capital	Male	100	110.94	9.757	2.475**
	Female	100	107.43	10.291	
Affective commitment	Male	100	37.44	7.382	2.227**
	Female	100	39.67	6.769	
Normative commitment	Male	100	36.47	6.386	3.084**
	Female	100	33.86	5.554	
Continuance commitment	Male	100	36.27	5.397	.156
	Female	100	36.39	5.451	
Quality of Work Life	Male	100	85.09	11.849	1.078
	Female	100	83.32	11.374	

***P<0.05*

The four independent sample t test was conducted to measure whether psychological capital, affective commitment, normative commitment, continuance commitment and quality of work life scores differ significantly between male and female school teachers. The result showed that there is significant difference in scores male and female school teachers in terms of psychological capital , affective and normative commitment.

Correlational Analysis

Table 4.4: Pearson correlation Coefficient between psychological capital and organizational commitment.

Variables	*Psychological capital*	*Affective commitment*	*Normative commitment*	*Continuance commitment*	*Quality of work life*
Psychological capital	1				
Affective commitment	.319**	1			
Normative commitment	.193**	.007	1		
Continuance commitment	.295**	.437**	.241**	1	
Quality of work life	0.535**	.452**	0.00	.234**	1

***P<0.05*

The Pearson correlation coefficient technique was applied to measure relationship between psychological capital, three dimensions of commitment and quality of work life. The results showed that there is significant positive correlation between organizational commitment and psychological capital life, all the three dimension of organizational commitment found to have significant positive correlation with psychological capital among the school teachers.There was significant positive correlation between psychological capital and Quality of Work Life. The quality of work life was found to have significant positive correlation between two dimensions of organisational commitment i.e. affective and continuance commitment.

Discussion

The present study was carried out to examine the relationship between psychological capital, organizational commitment and quality of work life among school teachers of Arunachal Pradesh. The study included 50% teachers from govt. school and 50% teachers from private school including both male and female teachers equally. The findings from descriptive analysis showed that psychological capital is above moderate level in both government and private school teachers. It was evident that three dimensions of organizational commitment are above moderate and quality of work life is moderate.

The findings from inferential statistics showed that continuance commitment differ significantly between government and private teachers. The findings showed that psychological capital, affective and normative commitment differ significantly between male and female teachers of Arunachal Pradesh. Previous literature supported this findings where studies by Marsden, et al. (1993) and Aftab et al. (2020) which also found significant difference between male and female in organizational commitmentshowed that men who work tend to have slightly greater levels of organizational commitment than women who work and also commitment to organization positively predicted citizenship conduct, and that when compared to male instructors, female teachers had higher levels of both dedication and citizenship behavior. Additionally, female teachers showed even better citizenship behavior at high organizational commitment levels. Another two studies by Feldman, K. (1993) and Kour, P. (2022) found significant difference between male and female in their psychological capital. Another study by Kour, P. (2022) indicates that psychological capital and well-being of workers in rural locations varied significantly based on gender. Married and single employees differ significantly in terms of psychological capital and well-being. Similary Feldman, K. (1993) shown that when gender disparities do occur, they tend to favour women slightly in overall student ratings of college teachers, despite the fact that studies generally indicate no significant differences in this regard

The findings from correlational analysis showed that all the three dimensions of organizational commitment positively correlated psychological capital and it was significant whereas only two dimensions of organizational commitment i.e. affective and continuance commitment was found to have significant positive correlation with quality of work life. The finding also showed that psychological capital was positively correlated to quality of work life and it was significant. This present finding can be supported by previous literature such as Paek, S., et al. (2015) in which also reported substantial relationship between higher psychological capital levels and better quality of work life and increased work engagement. Workers who scored highly on psychological capital expressed more job satisfaction, improved relationships with coworkers, and a happier workplace. Similarly Nafei, W. (2015) findings showed that Psychological capital and quality of work life is related and low Psychological capital can reduce knowledge and higher level can improve performance at work. The present study finding can be supported by Singh, P., & Chopra, R. (2018) which showed that quality of work life was greater among instructors in private schools, and that this was highly correlated with their Psychological capital scores as compared to public school teachers.

Conclusion

The present study concluded that psychological capital efficacy, hope, optimism and resilience are significantly correlated with organizational commitment and quality of work life among the school teachers at tribal communities. The study was able to address the gap identified in the area of psychological capital and contributed new findings in special context of teachers from tribal areas. The study highlighted the need o understand these variable in depth manners by qualitative approach in future.

References

Aftab, N., Shah, S., & Khan, Z. (2020).The moderating effect of gender on the relationship between organizational commitment and organizational citizenship behavior in Pakistani university teachers. *Cogent Psychology,* 7, https://doi.org/10.1080/23311908.2020.1860480

Awaliah, R., & Ingarianti, T. M. (2024).The relationship between psychological capital and career commitment in teachers. *Research and Development in Education (RaDEn),* 4(1), 709-724.

Çimen, I., & Özgan, H. (2018). Contributing and Damaging Factors Related to the Psychological Capital of Teachers: A Qualitative Analysis. *Issues in Educational Research, 28(2),* 308–328. https://www.iier.org.au/iier28/cimen.pdf

Clarence, M., Viju, P. D., Jena, L. K., & George, T. S. (2021). Predictors of Positive Psychological Capital: An Attempt Among the Teacher Communities in Rural Jharkhand, India. *Management and Labour Studies, 46(2),* 139–160. https://doi.org/10.1177/0258042X21991013

Feldman, K. (1993). College students' views of male and female college teachers: Part II—Evidence from students' evaluations of their classroom teachers. *Research in Higher Education,* 34, 151-211. https://doi.org/10.1007/BF00992161

Fischer, R., &Mansell, A. (2009). Commitment across cultures: A meta-analytical approach. *Journal of International Business Studies,* 40(8), 1339-1358.

Hansen, A., Buitendach, J. H., & Kanengoni, H. (2015).Psychological capital, subjective well-being, burnout and job satisfaction amongst educators in the Umlazi region in South Africa. *Journal of Human Resource Management,* 13(1), 1–9. https://doi.org/10.4102/SAJHRM.V13I1.621

Herrick, N. Q. (1981). The means and end of work. *Human relations,* 34(7), 611-632.

Jia, L., & Zhang, Q. (2024). Does the Psychological Capital of Government Employees Affect Job Performance? A Survey of 2357 Government Employees in China. https://doi.org/10.21203/rs.3.rs-4929087/v1

Kour, P. (2022). Psychological Wellbeing and Psychological Capital Among Teachers Working in Rural Areas. *International Journal of Indian Psychology,* 10(3), 1323-1331. doi:18.01.141.20221003, DOI:10.25215/1003.14

Meyer, J. P., Stanley, D. J., Jackson, T. A., McInnis, K. J., Maltin, E. R., & Sheppard, L. (2012). Affective, normative, and continuance commitment levels across cultures: A meta-analysis. *Journal of vocational behavior,* 80(2), 225-245.

Marsden, P., Kalleberg, A., & Cook, C. (1993).Gender Differences in Organizational Commitment. *Work and Occupations,* 20, 368 - 390. https://doi.org/10.1177/0730888493020003005

Nafei, W. (2015). Meta-analysis of the impact of psychological capital on Quality of Work Life and organizational citizenship behavior: A study on Sadat City University. *International Journal of Business Administration,* 6(2), 42.

Olanrewaju, M. K., & Tinuke, K. R. (2022). Psychological Capital and Quality of Life Among Secondary School Tutors in Kwara State Nigeria. *Journal of Psychological Perspective,* 4(1), 17–20. https://doi.org/10.47679/jopp.412072022

Perveen, Y., Raza, A., Khan, M.J., Matloob, S. and Jaboob, A.S. (2025), Burnout and Beyond: Exploring How Work Environment, Self-Efficacy, and Emotional Exhaustion and Job Security Drive Quitting Intentions Among Newly Recruited Teachers in Sindh, Pakistan. *Psychology in the Schools, 1-16,* https://doi.org/10.1002/pits.23564

Paek, S., Schuckert, M., Kim, T. T., & Lee, G. (2015). Why is hospitality employees' psychological capital important? The effects of psychological capital on work engagement and employee morale. *International journal of hospitality management, 50,* 9-26.

Sharma, S., & Sengupta, S. (2025). From pressure to progress: examining teaching demands and resources in Private Higher Education Institutes of India. *Higher Education Research & Development,* 1-15.

Singh, P., & Chopra, R. (2018). Quality of Work Life among teachers in private and government schools: Role of psychological capital. *Journal of Educational Psychology, 42(3),* 213-230.

Wasti, S. A., & Can, Ö. (2008). Affective and normative commitment to organization, supervisor, and coworkers: Do collectivist values matter?.*Journal of vocational behavior,* 73(3), 404-413.

Zhang, J., Zhang, J., Yan, Y., Tang, H., Luo, X., & Yang, W. (2024).The Power of Psychological Capital.*International Journal of Reproductive Research, 3(2).*https://doi.org/10.58489/2836-2225/024

2

Mental Health and Well-being: A Developmental Perspective on Education Scenario

Dr. G. Panneerselvam

Faculty on Mathematics (On contract), Department of Education,
National Institute of Technology Puducherry, Karaikal-609609
Email: reach2panneer@gmail.com

Abstract

This chapter examines the complex relationship between mental health and education, highlighting how psychological well-being has a significant influence on learners' academic outcomes and personal development. The work introduces the concept of mental health in educational settings and examines how learning environments are influenced by teachers' and students' perspectives on mental health. Thus this section also emphasizes the significance of students' mental health by outlining the current situation, which shows both advancements and ongoing difficulties in incorporating mental health awareness into educational systems. It looks at how mental health has two effects: while poor mental health degrades cognition, lowers academic performance, and raises absenteeism and dropout rates, good mental health improves cognitive function, motivation, perseverance, and stress management. As crucial elements of holistic education, the conversation continues to address the "wheel of well-being," elucidating its cognitive aspects and their relationship to mental health. The National Education Policy (NEP) 2020, which emphasizes the importance of comprehensive mental well-being initiatives in schools and universities, serves as another lens through which to view the significance of prioritizing mental health in educational policy. Finally, this chapter concludes by asserting that fostering mental health in education is not merely beneficial but essential for nurturing resilient, motivated, and successful learners.

Keywords: *Mental Health, Cognitive abilities, Anxiety and Stress.*

1. Introduction

Mental health can be described as how individuals think, feel, behave, and interact with peers and others. In the context of education, mental health pertains to a learner's ability to cope with stress and make decisions regarding their environment. Also, good mental health is essential for a learner's personal and educational development; it also affects how a person relates to others and involves themselves with their environment. Additionally, mental health pertains to a state of psychological well-being that enables one to cope with life's pressures, acknowledge their abilities, learn efficiently, excel in their assignment, and participate in community service. It exists on a complex continuum that varies in experience from individual to individual, with contradictory levels of difficulty and distress. Learners' mental health and well-being are crucial aspects of their personal growth and academic development.

The main focus of this chapter is on the mental health and well-being of learners. The characteristics of mental health, its variations, the impact on the person's mental state, contributing factors, the definition of well-being, and how well-being can mitigate the effects of compromised mental health will be discussed in the forthcoming sections.

2. Mental Health

2.1 Perception of mental health in education

Mental health in education generally pertains to how well an individual or learner's mental activity is supported in their environment. This encompasses sustaining effective daily activities and upholding rewarding relationships with peers and others. It also encompasses preserving the capacity to adjust to change and manage stress. Thus, mental health in education acknowledges that a student's mental well-being (encompassing emotional, psychological, and social dimensions) is vital for their academic success and overall development. This entails comprehending the effects of mental health on learning, behavior, and social exchanges within the school context.

Mental health within the educational context can greatly affect a learner's academic success and general well-being. Challenges related to mental health can result in problems with attention, concentration, and problem-solving, which can impact learning in the classroom and academic performance. On the other hand, a positive atmosphere for mental health can foster student achievement, joy, and education.

Family is the first socialization framework the child is exposed to. It is an important cornerstone for a child because attachment, emotions, personality traits, and behaviours emanate from the family. Right from the favorite dish preference to interest and social interaction all depend on this one unit. The next framework of socialization is school (education). This provides a plethora of opportunities and psychological space for holistic development. Community, from a developmental perspective, has a broader meaning. It may include the teachers connected over an academic year. In the aspect of novice learners in education, mental health involves recognizing the importance of emotional, psychological, and social well-being concerning student learning and development. Also, it acknowledges the social relationships, and overall success in education and life. Especially in a scholastic setting, it is well known that learners can show resilience. Their ability to recover from challenges and disappointments is remarkable. Nonetheless, certain risk factors can significantly affect a child's mental health. This chapter will examine some of the key contributions to a learner's mental health, the effects of each on development, and strategies for helping learners to flourish despite these influences.

Learners during school years move through different stages of development and experience various changes and challenges at each stage. Resolving the challenges and adapting to the changes in these aspects requires a positive state of mental health. However, due to individual differences, learners vary in their ways of adapting and coping with challenges. The influence of factors such as psychological, social, and environmental factors on mental health needs to be well documented for further navigation to have a brief idea of mental health in education. Relying on the three primary domains (factors) of mental health, there exists a multitude of sub-factors that contribute to mental well-being. Ultimately, positive mental health contributes to learners' academic success; without it, they may face adverse learning conditions. In an educational climate, the primary sub-factors influencing learners' mental health will be academic stress, learning environment, and social pressure. Mental health can be greatly affected by academic stress, resulting in various problems such as anxiety, depression, and lower self-esteem. Research indicates that learners who face significant academic stress are more prone to indicate diminished mental well-being, declining academic results, and increased likelihood of mental health issues. The environment of a school has a considerable effect on the mental health of learners. A well-being can be promoted by positive and supportive atmosphere, whereas a detrimental environment can give rise to greater anxiety, depression, and other mental health problems. It is essential for learners' mental health and academic success to create a safe, inclusive environment in which they feel supported and connected. Social pressures, especially those stemming from peers and the expectations of school and society, can greatly affect a student's mental health. These pressures—stemming from factors like academic performance, social fitting, and social media comparisons - can result in anxiety, depression, and other mental health problems. For learners to thrive, it is essential to establish a caring and supportive atmosphere and to offer them tools for dealing with the pressures they face.

Considering the aforementioned sub-factors of poor mental health, it appears that there are general issues at play, as well as a multitude of additional problems linked to the difficulties arising in learners' academic performance. These may be primarily based on the individual differences of the learners, as they are shaped by factors related to the effects of the learning environment. Considering the effects, one must examine the beneficial influence of good mental health and the detrimental effect of poor mental health; this analysis provides a precise depiction of the field of mental health in education.

2.2 Importance of mental health on learners

Mental health plays a vital role in overall well-being, especially for learners. Academic pressures, social expectations, and the challenges of moving into adulthood can greatly affect mental health. It is crucial to prioritize mental health in the lives of learners who grapple with mental health issues, as these challenges can hinder their academic success and complicate their relationships in various aspects. Learners who place importance on their mental health are more likely to excel academically, cultivate better relationships, and lead a more satisfying life. Here are several reasons why mental health is crucial for learners:

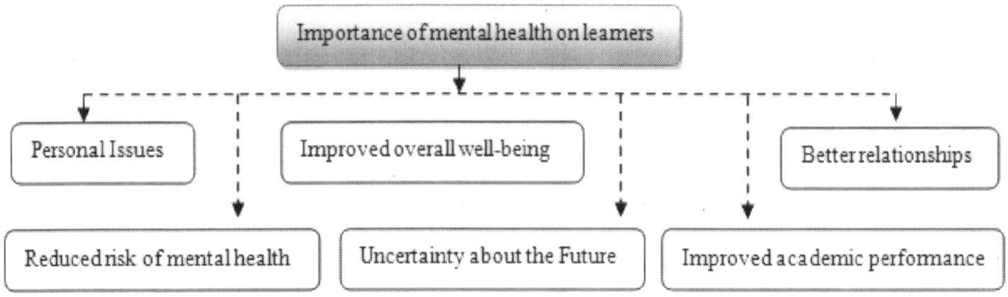

Figure: 1 Factors for importance of mental health on learners

The above figure 1 represents that the essential factors emphasizing the Factors for importance of mental health on learners. Each and every factor will be elaborated below. Improved academic performance: By giving priority to their mental health, learners are more capable of handling stress, anxiety, and depression. This can result in improved academic outcomes. Thus, the state of one's mental health has a considerable effect on academic performance. Learners who enjoy good mental well-being generally exhibit enhanced focus, concentration, and motivation, which contribute to improved academic performance. On the other hand, mental health challenges such as anxiety or depression can impair a learner's learning capacity, focus, and stress management abilities, thereby obstructing their academic advancement.

Enhanced relationships: Positive mental health can foster improved social connections and strengthen relationships with friends, family, and peers. Learning and relationships are significantly influenced by mental health. Positive mental health correlates with improved academic performance, enhanced social skills, and stronger relationships with teachers and classmates. On the flip side, problems related to mental health can obstruct learning, influence social relationships, and harm self-worth and general welfare.

Diminished risk of mental health issues: Learners who make their mental health a priority have a lower likelihood of developing issues like anxiety, depression, and substance abuse. A combination of strategies can achieve a low level of risk for learners' mental health issues, including creating a supportive school environment, promoting mental health literacy, and encouraging self-care and social connections. Schools and educators can assist students in building resilience and managing the challenges they encounter more effectively by adopting these strategies.

Enhanced overall wellbeing: Putting mental health first can contribute to improved overall wellbeing and a more satisfying life. For learners to achieve academic success, develop socially and emotionally, and maintain long-term health, their mental health and overall well-being must be prioritized. A nurturing and affirmative atmosphere can nurture mental wellbeing, resulting in enhanced learning outcomes, diminished stress levels, and heightened engagement.

2.3 Existing scenario

Especially since India's independence in 1947, the education system in India has changed multiple times over the last few decades. In the past, education was not given much attention because of assumptions such as that only certain people should study and that education is not meant for the poor. After the industry was liberalized in 1991, however, there was a resurgence of emphasis on establishing education as a national top priority. After 1991, the importance of enhancing India's extensive network of pre-primary schools, primary and secondary schools, colleges, state universities, central universities, and various national institutes became increasingly recognized. This was undertaken not only to attain the status of a prosperous nation but also to capitalize on the country's young demographic. Since that time, the education system has been developing in both rural and urban regions to ensure a better future for the country. A study on "Mental Health Problems in a School Setting in Children and Adolescents" by Schulte (2016) reported that the global prevalence of mental health problems of some type, affecting children and adolescents, is 10–20%.

Throughout childhood, an individual's mental health can be influenced by various factors. These may encompass genetic influences (such as a family history of mental illness), environmental influences (like exposure to trauma or abuse), and stress (from educational or familial challenges). It should be emphasized that not every child who encounters these factors will subsequently develop mental health issues. Nonetheless, these elements can heighten the risk for a child. Especially in an educational setup, attention deficits, cognitive disturbances, lack of motivation, and negative mood are all manifestations that negatively impact scholastic development. It is often unclear what factors associated with school affect children's mental development and what preventive measures and interventions at school might be effective.

Nowadays, learners in terms of accessing education must necessity to migrate, which can be regarded as the primary scenario that exposes them to mental health troubles. And this migration is a result of the situation regarding parental occupation or some personal consequence of the learner's familial setup. Similarly, the situation happens to exploring education and higher education, novice learners must navigate within national and global frameworks to access education in various contexts. So the learners need to catch up and adapt themselves to the new environment; failure leads to disturbance in their mental health. Since Mental health is a fundamental aspect of overall well-being, encompassing emotional, psychological, and social well-being. It is understood that schools and families serve as crucial social units that ground the health, mental health, and overall well-being of every individual. It is primarily the responsibility of schools to promote and optimize learners' physical, social, and mental health. Educational institutions have had to adjust their focus to encompass the psychosocial needs of learners and their overall well-being in light of the new challenges.

The mental health of novice learners is influenced by various factors within the current situation. To make more focus of this episode, this write-up focuses on the educational environment as one of these factors impacting learners' mental health, such as attention deficits, cognitive disturbances, lack of motivation, and negative mood, as discussed earlier.

3 The Impact of Mental Health on Education

Mental health significantly impacts positively and negatively the performance of learning in a scholastic setup. Good mental health can enhance focus, motivation, and coping abilities, leading to better academic outcomes for the learners. Conversely, poor mental health can negatively affect cognitive functions like memory and concentration, potentially leading to decreased academic performance and even dropout. Thus, the impact of mental health can be discussed with its dual side, positively and negatively, respectively.

3.1 Positive Impact of Good Mental Health

As discussed above, the impact of mental health in this sense has a dual perspective, it's positive and negative. A learner possessing good or positive mental health has no issues with their scholastic achievement; if found they can have resilience, and they can easily overcome the trouble without any negative impact. On the contrary, a poor or negative mental health of learners paves the way to numerous troubles in their educational progress. Thus, a theoretical overview of the dual perspective on mental health in education can be discussed herewith.

3.1.1 Improved Cognitive Function

Learners with good mental health can concentrate, remember information, and solve problems effectively—all of which are essential for academic success. As long as they do not encounter any difficulties in their learning, they can navigate their academic path without any interpretation. Enhanced cognitive function in education boosts different learning abilities, resulting in improved academic performance and overall cognitive growth. Thus, positive mental health plays a significant role in enhancing cognitive function. Through this, memory, concentration, attentiveness, and problem-solving are all necessary cognitive abilities that can be improved by a healthy mind.

3.1.2 Enhanced Motivation and Perseverance:

Learners who have a strong mental well-being are more inclined to maintain their motivation, endure difficulties, and reach their academic objectives. When an individual's motivation is boosted, it propels them to cultivate a greater impetus for positive change, which in turn betters their mental health. To facilitate enduring behavioral changes, this method concentrates on leveraging internal motivation instead of depending on external incentives or penalties. Additionally, perseverance in the realm of mental health denotes the capacity to continue striving for a goal in the face of challenges or difficulties. The focus is on sustaining motivation and exertion in tough times, as well as on drawing lessons from setbacks to make further attempts. For the development of resilience and for dealing with challenges that can affect mental well-being, perseverance is vital.

3.1.3 Reduced Stress and Anxiety

In the educational context, a positive mental state can assist learners in coping with academic pressures and mitigating the detrimental impact of stress on learning. Learner's mental health encompasses overall well-being, while it alleviates stress and anxiety, which are specific components that contribute to education. It is normal to feel stressed and anxious, but when these feelings become chronic and disrupt daily life, they can affect mental health. A crucial element in preserving good mental health is the reduction of stress and anxiety.

3.2 Negative Impact of Poor Mental Health

Learners' poor mental health can greatly affect their academic performance, social relationships, and overall well-being. It also obstructs their ability to succeed in education and other areas of life. This discussion will examine the adverse effects of poor mental health on learners, encompassing its impact on learning, school attendance, and social development.

3.2.1 Impaired Cognitive Abilities

Education can be greatly impacted by learners' cognitive impairments, such as learning disorders or cognitive impairments. Additionally, mental health issues like sadness and anxiety can affect one's ability to focus, remember things, and solve problems. These conditions lead to hindering academic performance and can affect various cognitive skills like attention, memory, and problem-solving, making it challenging for students to succeed academically. Educators can help by implementing strategies like positive reinforcement, checklists, task analysis, and special classroom accommodations.

3.2.2 Decreased Academic Performance

Poor mental health can lead to lower grades, difficulty completing assignments, and struggles with exams. It might be caused by conditions like stress, anxiety, and depression, which would have a big effect on academic performance. This is since these situations have the potential to impact motivation, focus, and general learning engagement. Research has indicated that unresolved emotional issues and ongoing stress might result in decreased academic engagement and attentiveness.

3.2.3 Increased Absenteeism and Dropout

Particularly in the post-COVID period, increased school absenteeism has a substantial negative influence on education and is closely associated with mental health problems. School absences are on the rise due to many factors, including mental health issues, lack of parental involvement, and a lack of effective government direction. As a result, absence can have a detrimental effect on learners' academic performance, including their capacity to participate in class activities and study for tests. Lastly, mental health problems might make learners feel overburdened and unable to go to class regularly, which may raise their chances of dropping out.

According to research, some groups—like young people who identify as sexual minorities—may have greater rates of anxiety and depression, which might cause them to miss more school because they are afraid or avoid them. Mental health issues affect people at all educational levels, from high school to college, and are a major contributing cause to school dropout.

4. The Wheel of Well-being

Learners' well-being serves as a vital protective barrier against the detrimental effects of mental health issues, enabling them to remain resilient and optimistic. For learners whose mental health is poor or negatively impacted by their education, the idea of wellbeing has been crucial. According to the opposing viewpoint, well-being is a viewpoint that may be examined from the perspectives of the social, physical, mental, and cognitive dimensions. The World Health Organization, on the other hand, uses the term well-being to define mental health as 'a state of well-being in which an individual realizes his or her abilities, can cope with the normal stresses of life, can work productively, and can contribute to his or her community. Therefore, rather of focusing on emotional, physical, and social well-being, it is crucial to focus on cognitive well-being in the effort to care for learners' well-being.

4.1 Well-being in a cognitive sense

In a cognitive sense, well-being can be termed as learners ' well-being, and its positive exposure is essential for learners if they have low or poor mental health. Cognitive mental health for a learner has come into play if the following conditions are met in the educational environment. Has the learner been able to concentrate and focus lately? Having trouble paying attention to their tasks? Is decision-making a challenge? and trouble with learn and recalling information easily? As a whole, cognitive wellbeing is an encompassing area of study that pertains to many aspects of wellbeing. It includes cognitive health, which is learning, memory, attention, thought, and language. Further, it's the evaluation of one's life and overall life satisfaction.

In a cognitive sense, well-being may be defined as learners ' well-being, and for those who are experiencing low or poor mental health. If the following criteria are satisfied in the learning environment, then a learner's cognitive and mental health is taken into consideration. Has the student recently been able to focus and pay attention? Having problems focusing on their work? Is making decisions difficult? And do you find it difficult to learn and remember information? All things considered, cognitive wellness is a broad field of study that touches on several facets of well-being. It encompasses cognitive health, which includes language, learning, memory, and attention. It also involves assessing one's life and general level of contentment.

4.2 Well-being and mental health

Everybody has mental health, and it can change every day. It might be more difficult to take action to improve one's welfare when one is not feeling well. Nonetheless, there are easy ways to take care of one's mental health. Learners who struggled academically because of poor mental health require assistance with their cognitive health. According to research, there are several advantages to taking action to promote wellbeing, including:

- Greater self-confidence in learning
- Improved quality in perception
- Healthier behaviors within peers
- Better understanding of cognitive concepts

As well as cognitive well-being and mental health are crucial for learners, as they directly impact learning outcomes and overall success. Strong mental health supports cognitive function, while cognitive skills are essential for learning and problem-solving. Therefore, a focus on both mental and cognitive well-being is vital for learners to thrive academically and emotionally.

5. Mental Health Well-being in Education Matters: Why?

In education, especially the young learners in there need to be more focus on it to perform well academically and to gain more knowledge. Fostering a comprehensive and encouraging learning environment requires that mental health and well-being be given top priority in the classroom. The government can provide a supportive environment that enables learners to flourish both academically and emotionally by de-stigmatizing mental health conditions, offering easily available assistance, and raising awareness. As a result, learners will get better results, feel more connected to the academic community, and become more resilient. Learners with good and positive mental health are better equipped to learn, focus, and engage with their studies reveals which positive mental health positively on academic success. In general, a learner with good mental health needs no care, and they can cope with their personality in education better. But the learners who have low or poor mental health need to be taken care of by their authorities. As was already said in the section above, learners who are experiencing mental health issues or who have been diagnosed with a mental health disease may find it difficult to focus, recall, and solve problems. They could also struggle to satisfy standards in the classroom. School personnel reprimand kids who are unruly, disinterested, or disrespectful. Academic performance is negatively impacted by exclusionary sanctions such as suspensions and expulsions. If learners are kept out of school, they are unable to participate and learn. Attendance and even graduation rates are impacted by a learner's mental health. To overcome these challenges, intervention programs on mental health for learners will encourage them to continue their education positively.

5.1 An accent in NEP 2020

The National Education Policy (NEP) 2020 acknowledges that learners' mental health and well-being are essential to their overall development and better learning outcomes. NEP 2020 proposes to address this by incorporating mental health into the curriculum, offering mental and emotional support through qualified experts, and establishing a supportive school atmosphere. This policy acknowledges that mental health is a critical component of total well-being and is necessary for high-quality learning. When learners are malnourished or ill, they cannot learn as effectively. Children's nutrition and health, especially mental health, will thus be addressed through the provision of nutritious meals, the integration of community engagement into the educational system, and the employment of qualified social workers and counselors.

Every learner will also be required to read excerpts from the Indian Constitution. The curriculum will also contain scientific explanations of the harmful effects of alcohol, tobacco, and other substances, as well as basic health education, including preventative health, mental health, proper nutrition, personal and public cleanliness, disaster response, and first aid. Therefore, when there are mental health problems brought on by the aforementioned reasons, the administrators of educational institutions should assume full responsibility for the students to advise and support their mental health.

6. Conclusion

Creating inclusive learning settings, including the merging of mental health education into the curriculum, is one way to overcome mental health issues by supporting well-being in education. To offer all-encompassing assistance, this entails educating the authorities in education and school personnel, creating mental health positions, and collaborating with neighborhood groups. Establishing welcoming and secure school settings is crucial to the long-term viability of education. Establishing a mental and physical space where children feel supported and protected should be a top priority for schools. This may entail putting policies in place to lessen exam and assessment-related anxiety. Giving the targeted learners access to clubs, organizations, and interest groups might help them participate in worthwhile activities that will improve their mental health and sense of belonging. They may therefore empower learners and increase their feeling of ownership in the educational system by encouraging them to take part in decision-making processes. Learners can gain a better understanding of mental health challenges, learn coping mechanisms, and lessen stigma by including mental health education within the core curriculum. Teachers who get training in mental health awareness and support techniques are more equipped to identify and meet the needs of their learners. Learners can benefit from specialized assistance and resources when mental health specialists are assigned to school settings. By addressing particular issues like separation anxiety, classroom settings that are pleasant, safe, and predictable can aid pupils in acclimating to the school setting. Exam anxiety can be decreased by implementing less demanding assessment methods, such as formative and peer evaluation. In addition to offering assistance for victims, schools must have explicit rules and processes in place for dealing with bullying and cyber bullying.

Overall, encouraging a pleasant school atmosphere and cultivating good connections between instructors and learners may result in caring. Mental health may be improved by including practices that support mental and physical well-being, such as mindfulness, exercise, and a good diet. Also, early learners who are at risk of mental health problems can be identified and supported with the implementation of early intervention programs. By putting these tactics into practice, schools may significantly contribute to the improvement of their students' mental health and general well-being, which will eventually create a more encouraging, welcoming, and productive learning environment.

References

Schulte-Korne G. (2016). Mental Health Problems in a School Setting in Children and Adolescents.DeutschesArzteblatt international, 113(11), 183–190.https://doi.org/10.3238/arztebl.2016.0183

https://manodarpan.education.gov.in/assets/img/pdf/CBSE_MH_Manual.pdf

https://academicstrive.com/CNNRIJ/CNNRIJ180064.pdf

https://www.education.gov.in/sites/upload_files/mhrd/files/NEP_Final_English_0.pdf

3

The Differential Impact of Intrinsic and Extrinsic Life Goals on Well-being among Students in Arunachal Pradesh

Dr. Dharmeshwari Lourembam[1] & Tarh Yaza[2]

[1]Assistant Professor & [2] Student, Department of Psychology, Rajiv Gandhi University, Doimukh, Arunachal Pradesh

Email: dharmeshwari.lourembam@rgu.ac.in

Abstract

Students are exposed to a multitude of stressors to cope with and so mental health of the student must be prioritized for a healthy and productive society. One's aspirations or life goals can be considered as one of the most important determinants It is thus pertinent to explore the life goals in the context to the well-being of the youth of Arunachal Pradesh. The present study examined the relationship between life goals (intrinsic & extrinsic) and satisfaction with life, positive affect, and negative affect on 100 college students, age ranging from 18 - 24 years. The Satisfaction with Life Scale, The Positive and Negative Affect Schedule and The Aspiration Index were administered. Results indicated that life goal of community showed a significantly positive relationship with both satisfaction with life and positive affect. Life goal for image was positive and significantly related to satisfaction with life while life goals of personal growth showed a significant negative relationship to negative affect.

Keywords: *Mental health, life goals, satisfaction with life, positive affect, negative affect.*

Introduction

Well-being is of paramount importance, especially for students in today's highly competitive and fast-paced society, as they are at a stage where they are grappling with many stressors ranging from academic, personal development, relationships and career. Deb et al.'s (2015) study on 190 Indian students also indicated that academic stress is a serious issue among the students. It further noted that parental pressure contributed to academic stress, which is further positively related to mental health issues. Further, the intense competition and peer pressure not only to perform academically but also to fit with the trend create a continuously demanding environment. After the Covid pandemic, the rapid and drastic penetration of the internet and social media has also exposed the students to a dynamic scenario to adjust. Thus, students are exposed to a multitude of stressors to cope with and so mental health of the student must be prioritized for a healthy and productive society.

A plethora of studies have focused on underscoring the factors related to the well-being of students or young adults. Among the wide range of psychosocial factors, one's aspirations or life goals can be considered as one of the most important determinants. One's life goals give motivation, purpose and direction, resulting in being the force behind the individual's thoughts and actions. Kasser and Ryan (1996) distinguished life goals as extrinsic goals consisting of goals for wealth, fame and image which is linked to some external rewards whereas intrinsic life goals consisting of personal growth, meaningful relationship and community feeling which are internally rewarding. Further, Ryan and Deci (2001) suggested that people who aspire for extrinsic goals are associated with lower psychological well-being and those who aspire for intrinsic life goals are associated with higher psychological well-being. Similarly, Yamaguchi and Halberstadt (2012) also highlighted the relationship between life goals and well-being among university students in New Zealand. Banth and Lourembam (2012) also conducted a study on Indian college students where intrinsic life goals were positively related to well-being, whereas extrinsic life goals were negatively related to well-being. Not only the type of aspiration one has but the attainment of life goals has also been linked to well-being. Emmons (2003) highlighted that the progress and commitment of goals were associated with positive affect and life satisfaction which are considered components of subjective well-being.

The impact of globalisation and modernisation is felt in every corner, and the tribal state of Arunachal Pradesh is not an exception. Arunachal Pradesh is one of the North-east states of India, which is home to more than a hundred tribes and sub-tribes which exhibit collectivistic values. In today's fast-changing society, a rapid change in lifestyle and values can also be seen among the people of the state. Although studies have documented the association of life goals and well-being; however, the focus on glamour and wealth in social media might have a deep impact, especially on the youth. It is thus pertinent to study the life goals in the context to the well-being of the youth of Arunachal Pradesh.

Objectives of the Study

1. To assess the level of life goals, satisfaction with life goals, positive affect and negative affect among students of Arunachal Pradesh.
2. To explore the relationship between life goals (intrinsic & extrinsic) and satisfaction with life.
3. To explore the relationship between life goals (intrinsic & extrinsic) and positive affect.
4. To explore the relationship between life goals (intrinsic & extrinsic) and negative affect.

Hypotheses

H1: There would be a positive relationship between intrinsic life goals and satisfaction with life.

H2: There would be a negative relationship between extrinsic life goals and satisfaction with life.

H3: There would be a positive relationship between intrinsic life goals and positive affect.

H4: There would be negative relationship between extrinsic life goals and positive affect.

H5: There will be a negative relationship between intrinsic life goals and negative affect.

H6: There will be positive relationship between extrinsic life goals and negative affect.

Methodology

Research design: It is a quantitative research which explores the relationship between life goals (intrinsic & extrinsic), satisfaction with life, positive affect and negative affect.

Sample: The sample consisted of students of Arunachal Pradesh who were enrolled in different colleges and belonged to different districts of the state. The study was conducted on 100 college students, aged between 18 - 24 years. Students from all the streams were included.

Tools:

i) The Satisfaction with Life Scale, developed by Diener et al. in 1985 was employed to evaluate satisfaction with life. This scale is considered to be a useful tool for assessing subjective well-being. It has 5 items which are to be rated from 1 (strongly disagree) to 7 (very satisfied). A higher total score indicates greater overall satisfaction with life, while a lower score suggests lower satisfaction. The scale has been widely used, including Indian population, showing good psychometric properties.

ii) The Positive and Negative Affect Schedule, developed by Watson et al. in 1988 is a widely used psychological tool to measure two distinct dimensions of emotional experience - positive affect and negative affect. It assesses an individual's subjective experiences of positive and negative emotions over a specified period, such as the past week. It consists of a list of adjectives representing positive emotions, such as joyful and enthusiastic, as well as negative emotions, such as nervous and irritable. Responses are taken on a Likert scale ranging from 1 (very slightly or not at all) to 5 (extremely). The scores are calculated separately, and higher scores on the positive affect scale mean greater positive emotional experience, whereas higher scores on the negative affect scale mean greater negative emotional experience.

iii) The Aspiration Index, developed by Kasser and Ryan in 1996, was used to measure the aspirations and goals across various domains of life, which are categorised as intrinsic and extrinsic life goals. The extrinsic life goals include wealth, fame and image while the intrinsic life goals include personal growth, meaningful relationship and community feeling. The index consists of items that ask respondents to rate the importance of specific aspirations to them personally on a scale, from 1 (not important at all) to 5 (extremely important). Higher scores indicate greater importance on those aspirations, suggesting stronger motivation to pursue them.

Data analyses: The data have been entered in IBM SPSS (Statistical Package for Social Science, Version 20) and analyses were conducted for Descriptive statistics (Mean and Standard Deviation), Correlation, and Stepwise Multiple Regression.

Result and Discussion

Table 1. ***Demographic details of the participants***

Characteristics	*Category*	*N*	*%*
Gender	Male	49	49%
	Female	51	51%
Age	17-20	59	59%
	21-24	41	41%
Semester	II	46	46%
	IV	31	31%
	VI	23	23%

The sample consisted of 51% females and 49% males, while in terms of age, 59% of the participants were 17-20 years and 41% were 21-24 years. A higher percent, i.e., 46% of the sample were studying in IInd semester, followed by 31% in IVth semester and 23% in VIthsemester.

Table 2. Mean, SD and Pearson Correlation of the Study Variables

Variables	*Mean*	*SD*	*1*	*2*	*3*	*4*	*5*	*6*	*7*	*8*	*9*
SWL	20.27	6.19	1								
PA	30.98	6.63	.360**	1							
NA	24.13	7.17	-.249*	.164	1						
LGW	18.91	3.31	-.038	.024	.086	1					
LGF	16.65	3.06	.182	.121	.130	.141	1				
LGI	16.52	2.82	.229*	-.011	.004	.086	.458**	1			
LGPG	19.43	2.56	.134	.004	-.207*	.256*	.055	.042	1		
LGA	17.48	2.89	.147	.177	.075	.320**	.461**	.341**	.288**	1	
LGC	19.87	2.88	.274**	.241*	.095	.229*	.416**	.223*	.278*	.121	1

*Correlation is significant at the 0.05 level.

** Correlation is significant at the 0.01 level.

***Note**: SWL=Satisfaction with life, PA=Positive affect, NA= Negative affect, LGW=Life goal of wealth, LGF=Life goal of fame, LGI=life goal of image, LGPG=Life goals of personal growth, LGA=Life goal of affiliation, LGC=life goal of community.*

The findings indicated that the life goal for image was positive and significantly related to satisfaction with life; however, previous studies highlighted a negative relation between extrinsic goals of image with satisfaction with life (Banth&Lourembam, 2012). This may be due to the changing meaning of image in today's scenario, which is highly influenced by social media, where image plays a nearly synonymous meaning to success. The way people surrounding you perceive and form your image has taken an important place in the youth's life. Further, life goals of personal growth showed a significant negative relationship to negative affect, indicating that those who focus on bringing out the best potential and work to improve their strengths experience fewer negative emotions. Another pertinent finding was that the life goal of community showed a significantly positive relationship with both satisfaction with life and positive affect. This implied that those who work for the collective good of their community and have strong commitment toward giving back to their society experienced satisfaction with life and positive emotions, such as joy, energetic, and happy. The positive relationship of intrinsic life goals and positive affect and negative relationship with negative affect have been well documented in previous studies (Ryan &Deci, 2001; Yamaguchi &Halberstadt, 2012; Banth&Lourembam, 2012). It thus clearly highlighted that focusing on one's intrinsic life goals positively contributed to one's well-being. The findings showed that all the hypotheses were accepted except H_2 in the case of life goals of image.

Table 3: Stepwise multiple regression for the criterion variable of Satisfaction with life and all six life goals as the predictor variables.

Model	*R*	*R^2*	*R^2 Change*	*F*	*Sig. F Change*	*beta*	*t*	*sig*
1	.274[a]	.075	.075	7.974	.006	.25	2.6	.01
2	.343[b]	.118	.042	4.654	.033	.21	2.5	.03

a. Predictors: (Constant), *Life goal of community*

b. Predictors: (Constant), *Life goal of community*, *Life goal of image*

The stepwise multiple regression table indicated that life goal of community came out as a predictor for satisfaction with life, explaining 7.5 % variance, and life goal of image also came out as a predictor for satisfaction with life, explaining 4.2% variance. Other life goals did not emerged as a significant predictor of satisfaction with life. This highlight the important role of life goals for contributing something towards one's community has an immense impact on the satisfaction with life. Further, life goals for one's image, that is, how other people perceive about them and the goal to make oneself stand out of the crowd also plays an important role in satisfaction with life.

Table 4. Stepwise multiple regression for the criterion variable of Positive affectand all six life goals as the predictor variables.

Model	*R*	*R^2*	*R^2 change*	*F*	*SIG. F change*	*beta*	*t*	*sig*
1	.241[a]	.058	.058	6.059	.016	2.4	2.5	.02

a. Predictors: (Constant), *Life goal of community*

The stepwise multiple regression indicated that life goal of community came out as a predictor for positive affect, explaining 5.8 % varianceshowing that aspiring to do or contribute something positive for the community plays an important role in one's experience of positive emotions and feelings.

Stepwise multiple regression for the criterion variable of Negative affectand all six life goals as the predictor variables.

Model	*R*	*R^2*	*R^2 change*	*F*	*SIG. F change*	*beta*	*t*	*sig*
1	.208[a]	.043	.043	4.419	.038	-.21	2.1	.04

a. Predictors: (Constant), *Life goal of personal growth*

The stepwise multiple regression table indicated that life goal of personal growth came out as a predictor for negative affect, explaining 4.3 %. As the beta value is negative, it indicated that life goals for one's growth and goals for bringing out one's best potential plays an important role in a person's feeling of less negative feelings and emotions. In other words, those who focus on the growth of his/her potential will feel less sad and jittery.

Conclusion

Life goals guide our behaviour and motivate to work in alignment to achieve them. Youth who aspire for intrinsic goals, that is, focus on personal growth, meaningful relationships and community feeling experience satisfaction with life and positive feelings. Intrinsic life goals are also related to the experience of fewer negative feelings. On the other hand, a focus on extrinsic life goals, like image, fame and wealth, is related to lesser positive emotions and more negative emotions. In the study, however, it was found that life goals of image were positively related to satisfaction with life, indicating that for the youth, the recognition and how people around you perceive you plays an important role in their sense of satisfaction. Youth must be made aware of the right way of interpreting attention in today's society of social media where getting recognition has been given too much importance. This information can be used in developing implementation programs for the youth for the enhancement of their well-being.

References

Deb, S., Strodl, E., & Sun, J. (2015).Academic stress, parental pressure, anxiety, and mental health among Indian high school students. *International Journal of Psychology and Behavioral Sciences, 5*(1), 26-34.

Emmons, R. A. (2003). Personal goals, life meaning, and virtue: Wellsprings of a positive life. In C. L. M. Keyes & J. Haidt (Eds.), Flourishing: Positive psychology and the life well-lived (pp. 105–128).American Psychological Association.

Kasser, T., & Ryan, R. M. (1996). Further examining the American dream: Differential correlates of intrinsic and extrinsic goals. Personality and Social Psychology Bulletin, 22(3), 280–287.

Ryan, R. M., & Deci, E. L. (2001). On happiness and human potentials: A review of research on hedonic and eudaimonic well-being. Annual Review of Psychology, *52*(1), 141–166.

Yamaguchi, M. & Halberstadt, J. (2012).Goals and well being in New Zealand. *New Zealand Journal of Psychology, 41*(2), 5-10.

4

Learning with Peace of Mind: Why Well Being Matters in Education

Kalpana Sarkar[1] & Dr. Sushant Kumar Nayak[2]

[1]*Research Scholar, Rajiv Gandhi University, Arunachal Pradesh*
[2]*Assistant Professor, Rajiv Gandhi University, Arunachal Pradesh*
Email: sushant.nayak@rgu.ac.in

Abstract

In recent years, mental health has gained significant attention. Mental health is a very crucial part of human life. It plays an important role in social, emotional and academic development, especially for students. Good mental health helps students to manage stress of life, build positive relationship with others, effectively perform own work and contribute to society. Most of the students are facing different types of mental health illness and these are neglecting in our society. If affects in our daily living. Poor mental health can lead less productivity and long term health issues. Through mental health awareness we can boost confidence, make oneself emotionally and mentally strong, improve creativity ability and improve our physical health. This paper tries to provide a brief introduction of mental health. Also this paper highlights the need and importance of mental health in educational setting. This paper discusses about different types of strategies which can enhance our mental health.

Keywords: *Mental Health, Education, Students, Mental illness*

Introduction

In the context of higher education, success doesn't only depend on intellectual capabilities and hard work, rather mental health is very crucial component of success. Teaching is a critical profession, where mental health problem is an ongoing issue but never studied. As a result, nowadays these issues are increasingly noticeable. These issues negatively affect both teaching and learning process (Joseph, 2023).

Mental health is a condition of well-being where a person can build a balanced personality, effectively manages stresses of life, stay productive and plays a meaningful role to society. It is necessary for personal well-being as well as for healthy community functioning (Das & Dhar, 2023). The importance of mental health has increasingly growing day by day in our society. Mental health refers to our emotional, social and psychological well-being. It reflects in how we think, what we feel and how we behave in our daily living. Mental hygiene is a way to maintain mental health (Rai et al. 2025). Mental health is become as a major issue in India. There are a lot of reasons which can hinder progress of mental health in our country such as giving less priority on mental health, low funding and lack of understanding about how mental health is connected with other health issues (Singh). Many students with mental illness do not get proper treatment, nearly two third of the total population do not get treatment for their mental illness all over the world. In United States, there is treatment available but students do not receive proper treatment of their mental illness. People who don't share their mental health issues often feel internal shame and scared of being judged by others (Shim et al. 2022). Stress, anxiety and depression are the main component of mental health illness (Ghazali et al, 2024). Mental health can occur seven percent global diseases and around 19% of total disability years. Good mental health is valuable and it can affect many outcome of our life positively. Poor mental health can lead to early death, reduced lifespan and increase chances of other illness (Kondirolli & Sunder, 2022). Mental health problems start at the early stages or preschool stages of a child. Also many studies have found that specially in developing countries, emotional and mental problems among preschool children are common. For these problems early support is very important but only few numbers of children can get help at the right time (Semiz, 2024).

Review of Related Literature

School should not only focus on students mental health issues but also help students personally and socially for their overall growth. There should be a new model which can separate mental wellness and overall wellbeing. Education should focus on helping students and health services should handle mental illness of students. Mental health and wellbeing must be known by all (Norwich et al, 2022). Mental health problems in India are bigger than just reported. Low reported cases can be seen because of low awareness, lake of treatment of mental health illness, belief in traditional healing and lake of government on mental health issues. Common symptoms like headache and tiredness also can lead to mental health illness (B. et al, 2013). Good mental health refers feeling good, handling stress, connected well with others and an enjoyable life. Sometimes teens may feel stress, anxiety and sadness. Support from family and friend is very important during adolescent period. Parental care and self-belief mostly affect teen mental health (Sankar et al, 2017). Emotional and behavioural problems of children are common in developing country and students do not get early support to overcome it. Family and school both have equal responsibility to help students to improve mental health (Semiz, 2024). Proper treatment of mental illness is not enough, prevention of mental illness also necessary part. There is a need of prevention of mental illness in all stages of life *i.e.* from early stage to adulthood. But it could be difficult due to lack of government funding and lack political support. Research suggested that there is need of team work to reduce mental health problems in a great extent (Jacka & Reavley, 2014). Mental health of students is increasing day by day. It is very important to support student's mental health in school. School should support students academically, emotionally and mentally. Schools are facing different types of challenges related to mental health. School should adopt useful curriculum and training programme for improvement (Chibb et. al., 2023). Maintaining a good mental health is very important for students. Mental health and mental illness are totally different things. Family, school and society have an important role in supporting student's mental health. Social change and COVID 19 factors can impact on student's mental health (Kalita, 2023). Mental and behavioural disorders are responsible for 12% of global diseases. Women, elderly and industrial workers have the high risk of mental diseases. They are facing challenges like stigma, weak political support and low awareness. We should improve our living condition and mental well-being by healthcare (B et. al., 2013). There is a strong bonding between mental health and emotional intelligence. Emotional intelligence skills help to support good mental health in human being. It can also improve individual health in a large extent. School should include emotional intelligence training and therapy to support good mental health among students (Kawino, 2024).

Objectives

The aim of this paper is to

- To discuss about mental health.
- To discuss about Need and importance of Mental Health on education.
- To discuss about **Strategies to Enhance Mental Health.**

Conceptual Background of Mental Health

In simple terms, mental health means feeling good, handling stress, effectively coping with others and work well (Das & Dhar, 2025). Good mental health is essential for success in school. Mental health issues like anxiety and depression can affect student's mental health. So teacher should have training on mental health to support students (Fei & Oyam, 2024). Most of the mental health issues begin before the age of 24. That's mean school and colleges have the major role to play (Singh). Students do not get enough support for their mental health in school. Only serious mental health issues are noticed and small issues are ignored. Confidence, manage emotions and feeling good are the support system of mental health not only treatment. School may add mental health education to curricula and try to reduce stigma, detect mental health problems early and improve overall well-being. For a good mental health, emotional and behavioural support in school is necessary (Kawino, 2024).

Factors affecting mental health

According to Learnyoga (n.d.) there are 5 factors that can affect mental health. These are given below-

1. Biological Factor:

Biological factors are linked with brain functioning, so this factor plays a very important role in mental health of human being. Genetics and physiological conditions affect our mental health in a great extent. Our genes play an important rolc in our mcntal health. Some genetic disorder makes depression, anxiety, bipolar disorder and schizophrenia in human. But it can't work alone effectively, it also react with environmental factor. "Neurotransmitters" is a complex chemical of our brain which helps to control our feelings and mood. If the level of this chemical is imbalanced then it can create problem such as anxiety and depression. Medicine can help to fix these types of problems. Hormones also have important impact on our mental health.

2. Environmental Factor:

Environmental factors also can influence our mental health. Love, care, neglect and abuse these childhood experiences shape our feelings. Trauma can leave a deep effect in our life. Poor socio economic condition can cause stress. Having support and big changes in our life can also affect our mental health.

3. Lifestyle Factor:

Our way of living also can affect our mental health. Healthy eating habit and proper nutrition help us having healthy mental health. Physical activity makes us both mentally and physically strong. Good sleep is also essential for us. But harmful substances can damage our mental health.

4. Psychological Factor:

Thoughts and feelings also have a big contribution in mental health. Our coping capability with others affects how we feel. Good self-esteem makes us look confident. Our thinking pattern reflects in the way we think that can be positive or negative and this can affect our mental well-being.

5. Cultural and Societal Factor:

Cultural and Societal Factor affect our mental well-being in many ways. Stigma and discrimination make people feel afraid or ashamed to get their rights. Cultural norms and beliefs also affect persons understanding and trust. Media and technology can both positively and negatively affect a person.

Need and importance of Mental Health on education:

Mental health is a very important part of education system. It helps students to learn well and grow well. Good mental health help students to stay focused, calm mind and ready to learn in the classroom. Students with good mental health can easily handle stress, they can build strong friendship and they have more positive attitude than others. According to Kalita (2023), some need and importance of mental health on education are given below:

1. Building a Desirable Personality

Good mental health plays a significant role in building well-balanced and healthy personality of each student. Good mental health allows students to maintain their own need along with fit into society.

2. Helps in Proper Emotional Development

There is a deep relationship between mental health and emotional behavior of a person. Person having good mental health always show emotional maturity and stability in different situation. They can effectively manage with stress of life, control impulses and can express their feelings in a healthy way. Emotional stability helps people to stay calm in challengeable situation and helps to take right decision in tough situation.

3. Help in Proper social Development

Good mental health is a key to build healthy social relationship. When someone feels confident from inside and feels calm they can connect with others happily. It can help to adjust with social situation and show respect, patience and kindness to other people. It helps to improve communication skill, teamwork and respect to others feelings.

4. Help in Proper moral Development

People with good mental health always follow moral values and society norms. They can differentiate between right and wrong decision. They are honest and maintain the rules of society.

5. Helps in actualizing one's potentialities

People with good mental health can understand their full potential. When children understand themselves they are more likely to grow their abilities. On the other hand, children with poor mental health finding difficulties to understand own potential also they are always confused about their decision.

6. Helps in seeking proper adjustment

A mentally healthy adjusted person can positively deal with every situation in life. They can easily handle life's ups and downs and adjust with newness. It will help them to make a happy and successful life.

7. Helps in seeking Goals of Life

Good mental health helps people to work on their life goals in a right way. They feel motivated and confident. This helps them to stay positive, face challenges and do not give up easily. It can build discipline and self-belief within a person which can help to stay on the right path.

8. Helps in the prevention of mental illness

Good mental health protects a person from various types of mental illness. People with poor mental health can feel stress in life, loss and unexpected breaking down. Mentally healthy persons are better at building support, managing emotions and stay hopeful.

Strategies to Enhance Mental Health:

Mental health is a key part of overall development of human being; it can affect our lifestyle and mindset. Most of the people are facing emotional and mental challenges and it negatively influenced their life or reduces their work potential. Therefore it is become very important to strengthen and protect our mental health by using right strategy. Applying and understanding these strategies can be highly beneficial for our mental health. According to Medline Plus, n. d some of the strategies are mention here-

1. **Stay physically active:** Physical exercise is one of the most effective ways to boost mental health. Physical exercise can reduce feelings of stress by releasing endorphins, it is a chemical which can make us feel happier and relaxed.
2. **Get enough sleep:** Sleep has a strong impact on our mental health. Without proper sleep we can easily become annoyed and feel angry. Lack of sleep can increase depression. So make sure that we must have proper sleep schedule and get enough sleep.
3. **Eat a balanced diet:** Eating healthy food helps us to feel good and happier and less worried. Lack of eating balanced diet can create vitamin deficiency, which can affect both physical and mental health. Balanced diet gives us proper energy which our body requires for healthy development.
4. **Connect with others:** For a good mental health social connections and good relationship with others is essential. Others presence and support can reduce stress level. For a healthy social relationship we can spend time with our family or friends also can engage in community activities.
5. **Developing sense of purpose in life:** We can find our purpose of life in our job, learning new things and in exploring spiritual belief. Creative activities also provide a strong sense of purpose in our life. These actions can boost confidence and also can improve mental health.
6. **Meditation:** Meditation is a mind and body practice, which gives the power to control our mind. Also it can help to improve our concentration ability. It helps to staying calm and maintains our mental and emotional well-being.
7. **Developing coping skills:** Coping strategies are effective ways to deal with our stress. It helps to stay calm, face day to day life problems and take action. Some example of coping strategies are talking with someone, going for a walk, taking a break and taking deep breath.

Conclusion

A mentally healthy person can cope with every tough situation. For healthy and enjoyable life good mental health is essential component (Kalita, 2023). Mental health education helps to increase awareness about mental health and also helps to reduce stigma (Shim et al, 2022). In present decade, mental health and well-being education has become a necessary part of education system to maintain a healthy and peaceful life. It helps to reduce behavioural problems in children through school counseling process (Chibb et al, 2023). Government provides short time funding for mental health problems but it is not enough to see the real benefits in the field of mental health. There is need of long term follow up to permanently solve these problems. Some mental health problems come from outside the health system and these become difficult to prevent. So it becomes very important to work together with strong government policies to reduce mental health problems (Jacka&Reavley, 2014).

References

B, V., Gupta, A., Lohiya, A., & Kharya, P. (2013). Mental Health Issues and Challenges in India: A Review. *International Journal of Scientific and Research Publications, 3*(2), 1-3.

Chibb, M., Fatima, N., &Akhter, S. (2023). Education and Mental Health: A Review. *The International Journal of Indian Psychology, 11*(3), 2398-2406. DOI: 10.25215/1103.225

Das, D., & Dhar, D. (2023). Impact of Mental Health on Academic Achievement- A Qualitative Study. *International Journal of Research Publication and Reviews, 4*(8), 2833-2840.

Fei, C., & Oyam, D. M. (2024).The Role of Teacher Training in Addressing Student Mental Health Issues in the Classroom. *International Journal of Social Science and Humanities Research, 12*(2), 313-318. DOI: https://doi.org/ 10.5281/ zenodo.12591677

Ghazali, N. M. B., Sharif, N. F. B. M., Ismail, J., & Azizan, I. S. (2024). Mental Health Awareness Among Students in Higher Education. *Journal of Administrative Science, 21*(1), 189-213.

Jacka, F., & Reavley, N. (2014). Prevention of mental disorders: Evidence, challenges and opportunities. *BMC Medicine,* 12, 75.https://doi.org/10.1186/1741-7015-12-75

Joseph, V. (2023). The Impact of Mental Health on Academic Performance: A Comprehensive Examination. *Journal of Mental Health Issues and Behavior, 3*(6), 1-10. https://doi.org/10.55529/jmhib.36.1.10

Kalita, P. (2023). The Importance of Mental Health of Student in the Present Modern Context. *International Journal for Multidisciplinary Research, 5*(2), 1-9.

Kawino A. A. (2024). Enhancing Mental Health Support Systems in Schools: Strategies, Challenges, and Best Practices. *Research Invention Journal of Research in Education, 3*(2), 69-78.

Kondirolli, E., & Sunder, N. (2022). Mental health effects of education. Health Economics, 31(S2), 22–39. https://doi.org/10.1002/hec.4565

Learnyoga.(n.d.). What are the factors that affect mental health? Complete guide. SlideShare.https://www.slideshare.net/slideshow/what-are-the-factors-that-affect-mental-health-complete-guide/270393194

MedlinePlus.(n.d.).How to improve mental health. National Library of Medicine. Retrieved August 11, 2025, from https://medlineplus.gov/howtoimprovementalhealth.html

Norwich, B., Moore, D., Stentiford, L., & Hall, D. (2022). A critical consideration of 'mental health and wellbeing' in education: Thinking about school aims in terms of wellbeing. *British Educational Research Journal,* 00, 1– 18.https://doi.org/10.1002/berj.3795

Rai, N., Vedant., Kumar, U. (2024). THE ROLE OF MENTAL HEALTH AND HYGIENE IN EDUCATION. *International Journal of Creative Research Thoughts, 12*(7), 784-791.

Sankar, R., Wani, M. A., & R, I. (2017).Mental Health among Adolescents. *The International Journal of Indian Psychology,* 4(3), 15-21. DOI:10.25215/0403.102

Semiz, M. (2024). Promotion and Prevention of Mental Health in Early and Preschool Age: Status and Future Directions. *Anatolian Journal of Mental Health, 2*(1), 41-71.

Shim, Y. R., Eaker, R. & Park, J. (2022). Mental Health Education, Awareness and Stigma Regarding Mental Illness Among College Students. *Journal of Mental Health and Clinical Psychology, 6*(2), 6-15.

Singh, A. Mental Health in Academic Settings. *International Journal of Policy Sciences and Law, 1*(2), 481-501.

5

The Hidden Cost of Punishment: Effects on Mental Health and Classroom Climate

Himjyoti Medhi

Ph.D. Research Scholar,
Mahapurusha Srimanta Sankaradeva Viswavidyalaya, Nagaon
Email: himjyotimedhi14@gmail.com

Abstract

Disciplinary practices in educational settings, particularly those rooted in punitive approaches, often aim to maintain order and enforce behavioural standards. However, such methods can carry unintended psychological and environmental consequences. This study explores the hidden costs of punishment-based discipline on students' mental health and its broader impact on the classroom climate. Drawing on recent research and observational data, the paper examines how repeated exposure to punitive measures—such as verbal reprimands, isolation, and corporal punishment—can lead to increased anxiety, diminished self-esteem, and disengagement from learning. Furthermore, the study highlights how such practices may contribute to a culture of fear, reduce peer collaboration, and weaken teacher-student relationships. By critically analyzing these outcomes, the paper advocates for a shift toward more restorative and empathetic approaches to classroom management that prioritize emotional well-being and a supportive learning environment. The findings aim to inform educators, policymakers, and school leaders on the importance of balancing discipline with compassion to foster healthier and more effective educational spaces.

Keywords: *Punishment, Effects on mental health and classroom climate.*

Introduction:

Discipline has long been regarded as an essential component of effective teaching and classroom management. For decades, educators have relied on punitive measures such as scolding, detention, physical punishment, or exclusion - as tools to correct student behaviour and uphold institutional norms. While these strategies may yield short-term compliance, they often overlook the deeper psychological and emotional consequences for students. Emerging research in educational psychology and child development reveals that punishment, especially when harsh or frequent, can adversely affect students' mental well-being, erode their self-worth, and disrupt the overall learning environment.

In many classrooms, particularly in under-resourced or high-stress contexts, punitive discipline is still a dominant response to behavioural issues. However, its widespread use raises critical concerns: What messages do students internalize when punishment is the primary mode of correction? How does it shape their perception of authority, learning, and themselves? Moreover, what kind of classroom atmosphere does it cultivate for both the punished and their peers?

This paper seeks to unpack these questions by exploring the hidden psychological toll of punitive discipline and its broader implications for classroom climate. By examining the intersection between disciplinary practices, student mental health, and the socio-emotional dynamics of the classroom, this study aims to challenge traditional notions of control and advocate for more constructive, empathetic, and inclusive approaches to behaviour management in schools.

Internalized Messages: What Do Students Learn from Punishment?

When punishment is the dominant strategy used to manage behaviour in the classroom, students often internalize more than just a lesson about rules—they absorb messages about their worth, identity, and role within the school community. Rather than fostering self-discipline, frequent punitive responses can lead students to believe that they are inherently "bad" or incapable of positive change. This perception is especially damaging in younger children, whose self-concept is still developing.

Students may also learn to associate education with fear and control rather than curiosity and growth. Instead of reflecting on their behaviour and learning from it, they might focus on avoiding punishment, which stifles intrinsic motivation and critical thinking. In some cases, repeated punishment can lead to a learned helplessness, where students disengage completely, feeling that no matter what they do, they will be met with negative consequences.

Moreover, the message conveyed through punishment often lacks clarity. Without proper communication and emotional support, students may not fully understand why their behaviour was inappropriate or how to correct it constructively. This can create confusion, resentment, or even defiance, particularly among students who face additional stressors outside of school.

Shaping Perceptions: Authority, Learning, and Self-Identity

The use of punishment as a primary disciplinary tool significantly influences how students perceive authority figures, the learning process, and their own self-worth. In environments where punishment is frequent or harsh, students often come to view authority as synonymous with control, fear, and power rather than guidance, support, and fairness. This perception can hinder the development of healthy relationships with teachers and other figures of authority, making students less likely to seek help, express their opinions, or engage openly in classroom discussions.

In terms of learning, punitive environments can turn education into a source of stress rather than inspiration. When students associate school with the risk of being embarrassed, isolated, or penalized for mistakes, they may become reluctant to participate or take academic risks. This fear-driven atmosphere discourages curiosity, experimentation, and critical thinking—key components of meaningful learning. Instead of seeing errors as opportunities to grow, students may begin to fear failure and prioritize compliance over understanding.

Punishment also affects how students view themselves. Repeated negative feedback, especially when not accompanied by constructive guidance, can lead students to internalize labels such as "troublemaker" or "failure." Over time, this shapes their self-concept and may result in a fixed mindset, low self-esteem, and disengagement from school altogether. For marginalized or struggling students, this impact is often amplified, contributing to cycles of exclusion and underachievement.

Ultimately, when punitive discipline dominates classroom culture, it shifts the focus from learning and development to control and obedience. This not only undermines students' academic potential but also stifles their emotional and social growth.

The Ripple Effect: Classroom Atmosphere for the Punished and Their Peers

Punishment in the classroom does not affect only the individual student being disciplined- it reverberates through the entire classroom, shaping the collective atmosphere. When punitive measures are a regular feature of classroom management, the learning environment often becomes tense, anxious, and emotionally unsafe for all students.

For the student being punished, the classroom can quickly transform into a space of public humiliation and fear. Feelings of shame, isolation, and resentment are common, especially when punishment is carried out in front of peers. This not only damages the punished student's self-confidence but also increases the likelihood of withdrawal, behavioural escalation, or oppositional attitudes.

For their peers, witnessing frequent punishment can generate a sense of unease and fear. Students may become overly cautious, worried about making mistakes or attracting negative attention from the teacher. In such climates, participation tends to decrease, as students fear criticism or discipline. This stifles creativity, collaboration, and open communication—key elements of a healthy learning environment.

Moreover, a punitive classroom can foster a culture of competition and blame rather than cooperation and empathy. Students may begin to distance themselves from those who are often punished, leading to social fragmentation and exclusion. The trust between students—and between students and the teacher can erode, undermining the sense of community and shared purpose essential for effective learning.

In contrast to a supportive classroom where mistakes are treated as learning opportunities, a punishment-centred environment often prioritizes obedience over understanding. As a result, students may follow rules out of fear rather than respect or internal motivation, which is less sustainable in the long term.

Alternative Approaches to Discipline: Building Supportive Classrooms

In response to the growing body of evidence on the negative effects of punishment-based discipline, many educators and researchers advocate for alternative approaches that emphasize empathy, accountability, and positive relationships. These methods aim not only to manage behaviour but also to nurture students' emotional and social development while creating a respectful and inclusive classroom environment.

1. Restorative Practices

Restorative practices focus on repairing harm rather than punishing wrongdoing. Rooted in community-based conflict resolution models, this approach encourages dialogue, empathy, and mutual understanding. When a behavioural incident occurs, students are invited to reflect on their actions, understand their impact on others, and actively participate in resolving the issue. This promotes responsibility and helps students develop conflict-resolution skills. Teachers who use restorative circles, peer mediation, and facilitated conversations often report stronger classroom relationships and fewer repeat incidents.

2. Positive Behaviour Interventions and Supports (PBIS)

PBIS is a proactive, school-wide approach to behaviour management that reinforces positive behaviours rather than focusing solely on negative ones. Through clear expectations, consistent routines, and positive reinforcement, PBIS helps create a structured and supportive learning environment. Rather than reacting to misbehaviour with punishment, teachers provide feedback, encouragement, and targeted support to help students meet behavioural goals. Studies have shown that PBIS not only reduces disciplinary referrals but also improves academic outcomes and school climate.

3. Social-Emotional Learning (SEL)

Integrating Social-Emotional Learning into the curriculum equips students with essential skills such as self-awareness, self-regulation, empathy, and responsible decision-making. SEL programs foster emotional intelligence and interpersonal competence, which can significantly reduce disruptive behaviour and enhance classroom cohesion. When students are taught how to manage emotions, resolve conflicts, and build healthy relationships, they are more likely to engage positively with peers and teachers.

4. Trauma-Informed Teaching

Many behavioural issues stem from underlying trauma or chronic stress. Trauma-informed teaching recognizes this and encourages educators to approach student behaviour with sensitivity and care. Instead of viewing misbehaviour as defiance, teachers are trained to see it as a communication of unmet needs or emotional distress. This approach emphasizes safe, predictable environments and supportive adult relationships, which are crucial for helping students feel secure and ready to learn.

Unveiling the Impact: How Punishment Shapes Minds and Classrooms

The analysis of data gathered from teacher interviews, student reflections, and classroom observations reveals several key insights into the psychological and environmental consequences of punitive discipline in school settings. This can be discussed as below-

1. Emotional Distress and Fear-Based Compliance

Students who were frequently subjected to punishment reported feelings of anxiety, embarrassment, and low self-esteem. Many expressed that disciplinary actions, especially public scolding or physical punishment, left them feeling humiliated and afraid to participate in class. Teachers also observed that such students often became quieter, disengaged, or disruptive over time. These findings align with existing literature that associates punishment with heightened emotional distress and avoidance behaviours rather than genuine behavioural improvement.

2. Breakdown of Teacher-Student Trust

A significant theme across both student and teacher responses was the erosion of trust. Students who experienced punitive discipline described their teachers as unapproachable or unfair, often perceiving them as figures of authority rather than support. This breakdown in trust discouraged open communication, making students less likely to seek academic or emotional help. Teachers, in turn, noted difficulties in managing classroom relationships when punitive actions created a divide between them and their students.

3. Negative Peer Dynamics and Social Stigma

Punishment not only affected individual students but also altered peer relationships. Students who were regularly disciplined were often stigmatized by their classmates, leading to isolation and diminished peer support. In some cases, classmates expressed fear of being associated with punished students, further fragmenting classroom cohesion. These social consequences contributed to a hostile and judgmental classroom environment, where collaboration and inclusivity were compromised.

4. Suppression of Intrinsic Motivation

Observations showed that students in punishment-heavy classrooms tended to follow rules out of fear rather than internalized values. Their motivation to learn was tied to avoiding negative consequences, not personal growth or curiosity. Teachers shared concerns that students became compliance-driven rather than engaged learners, often prioritizing obedience over meaningful participation or critical thinking.

5. Positive Impact of Restorative and Supportive Approaches

In contrast, classrooms that implemented restorative and positive behaviour strategies demonstrated stronger student-teacher relationships and more inclusive classroom cultures. Teachers reported fewer repeated behavioural issues and greater student willingness to reflect on and correct their actions. Students in these environments described their classrooms as safe, respectful, and emotionally supportive, allowing them to take academic risks and form meaningful peer connections.

Conclusion

The evidence presented throughout this study underscores a critical reality: punishment-based discipline, while often intended to enforce order, carries significant emotional and relational costs for both students and the wider classroom community. Rather than fostering responsibility and growth, punitive practices frequently result in fear, disengagement, and damaged self-perception. The classroom, instead of being a space for exploration and collaboration, becomes a place of control, anxiety, and silence.

Importantly, the effects of punishment extend beyond the individual. They shape the overall classroom atmosphere—weakening trust, stifling peer relationships, and suppressing intrinsic motivation. These outcomes are particularly concerning in environments where learning thrives on connection, safety, and open communication.

Ultimately, rethinking discipline is not about removing structure, but about rebuilding it on foundations of respect, empathy, and emotional intelligence. For schools to be truly nurturing and transformative spaces, educators must move beyond the logic of punishment and embrace strategies that honour the dignity and potential of every learner.

References

Bear, G. G. (2010). Discipline: Effective school practices. National Association of School Psychologists.

Gershoff, E. T., & Grogan-Kaylor, A. (2016). Spanking and child outcomes: Old controversies and new meta-analyses. *Journal of Family Psychology, 30*(4), 453–469. https://doi.org/10.1037/fam0000191

Gregory, A., Clawson, K., Davis, A., & Gerewitz, J. (2016).The promise of restorative practices to transform teacher-student relationships and achieve equity in school discipline. *Journal of Educational and Psychological Consultation, 26*(4), 325–353. https://doi.org/10.1080/10474412.2014.929950

Pianta, R. C., & Hamre, B. K. (2009). Conceptualization, measurement, and improvement of classroom processes: Standardized observation can leverage capacity. *Educational Researcher, 38*(2), 109–119. https://doi.org/10.3102/0013189X09332374

Skiba, R. J., & Losen, D. J. (2016). From reaction to prevention: Turning the page on school discipline. *American Educator, 39*(4), 4–11. https://www.aft.org/ae/winter2015-2016/skiba_losen

Thapa, A., Cohen, J., Guffey, S., & Higgins-D'Alessandro, A. (2013). A review of school climate research.*Review of Educational Research, 83*(3), 357–385. https://doi.org/10.3102/0034654313483907

Van der Kolk, B. (2014). The body keeps the score: Brain, mind, and body in the healing of trauma. Viking.

Wachtel, T. (2016).Defining restorative.International Institute for Restorative Practices. https://www.iirp.edu/images/pdf/Defining-Restorative_Nov-2016.pdf

6

The Tech Effect: Exploring the Impacts of Digital Technologies on the Emotional Health of Adolescents

Mandakini Deka

Ph.D. Research Scholar,
Mahapurusha Srimanta Sankaradeva Viswavidyalaya, Nagaon
Email: deka.mandakini@gmail.com

Abstract

In an increasingly digitized world, adolescents are growing up immersed in digital technologies that profoundly shape their emotional landscapes. This study explores the complex relationship between digital technology use and emotional health in adolescents. Multifaceted impact of digital technologies including social media, gaming, mobile apps, and virtual interactions has great impacts on the emotional health of adolescents. While digital tools offer opportunities for self-expression, social connectivity, and access to mental health resources, they also present significant risks such as cyberbullying, social comparison, digital addiction, and sleep disruption. Drawing on recent interdisciplinary research from psychology, education, and digital media studies, this paper examines both the positive and negative consequences of technology use among youth. Finally, this paper calls for a balanced approach to technology use that safeguards adolescent mental well-being without disregarding the potential benefits of digital engagement.

Keywords: *Digital Technology, Emotional Health and Adolescents*

Introduction

Adolescence is a critical period of emotional development, marked by heightened sensitivity to social experiences, identity formation, and the need for belonging. Digital technologies have become integral to how adolescents communicate, learn, socialize, and even cope with stress. While these tools can foster creativity, provide emotional support, and bridge geographical distances, they also carry inherent risks that can adversely affect emotional health. Issues such as cyberbullying, social comparison, digital overuse, and online peer pressure have been linked to rising rates of anxiety, depression, loneliness, and body image concerns among adolescents. Conversely, online communities and digital interventions have shown promise in supporting youth mental health through access to resources, peer support, and therapeutic tools.

Digital Addiction and the Mental Health of Adolescents

Digital addiction is a term that is characterized by excessive and compulsive use of digital devices such as smartphones, social media platforms, and gaming systems etc. Which has emerged as a significant mental health concern among adolescents now a days. This behavioural pattern often disrupts sleep, social relationships, academic performance, and emotional well-being, creating a cycle that is difficult to break.

Adolescents are particularly vulnerable due to their still-developing self-regulation skills and heightened sensitivity to peer approval. Social media platforms exploit these psychological traits through algorithms that encourage endless scrolling, instant feedback (likes, comments), and fear of missing out (FOMO). As Dr. Jean M. Twenge, a psychologist and author of iGen, states , "*There is a significant correlation between the amount of time teens spend on screens and their levels of happiness, and that correlation is negative. Teens who spend more time on screen activities are more likely to be unhappy, and those who spend more time on non-screen activities are more likely to be happy.*"

Digital addiction has been linked to increased rates of depression, anxiety disorders, attention problems, and low self-esteem in adolescents. Sleep deprivation caused by late-night screen use can further exacerbate emotional instability. Moreover, constant exposure to curated lives on social media can lead to feelings of inadequacy and social comparison. In response to this growing concern, psychologists advocate for digital hygiene practices, such as setting screen-time limits, encouraging tech-free zones at home, and promoting offline hobbies and peer interactions.

Adolescents' Perceptions of the Benefits and Limitations of Online Support Systems for Emotional Well-Being:

Adolescents today increasingly turn to online support systems- such as mental health apps, peer forums, Chabot's, and social media communities- to seek emotional support, share experiences, and find a sense of belonging. Many perceive these platforms as safe spaces where they can express vulnerabilities anonymously, without fear of judgment or stigma often present in face-to-face interactions. For instance, mental health apps like Calm, Woebot, or 7 Cups offer structured tools for anxiety management, mood tracking, and even real-time emotional guidance, which adolescents often find convenient, private, and empowering. Online communities, such as Reddit's mental health subreddits or Instagram pages focused on self-care, allow teens to feel seen and validated by peers facing similar challenges. However, while these platforms offer accessibility and immediacy, adolescents are also increasingly aware of their limitations. Many express concern over the lack of professional oversight, the risk of misinformation, and the potential for toxic or triggering content within unmoderated spaces. Moreover, some teens report feeling overwhelmed or invalidated when their experiences are met with generic advice or insincere responses. The blurred lines between genuine empathy and superficial interactions can sometimes lead to deeper feelings of isolation. Additionally, the constant availability of online help may discourage seeking in-person therapeutic support, which is often more effective for complex emotional needs. Thus, while adolescents appreciate the accessibility and anonymity that online support systems provide, they also acknowledge the need for more reliable, empathetic, and professionally guided digital spaces to truly enhance their emotional well-being.

The Role of Parental Guidance and Monitoring in Mitigating the Negative Effects of Technology on Adolescent Emotional Health

Parental guidance and monitoring play a crucial role in protecting adolescents from the potential emotional and psychological harms of excessive or unhealthy technology use.While digital devices offer adolescents opportunities for learning, socializing, and creative expression, unsupervised or unregulated access can lead to increased risks of cyberbullying, exposure to inappropriate content, social isolation, and symptoms of anxiety and depression. Active parental involvement- such as setting screen-time limits, co-viewing content, discussing digital experiences, and modeling healthy tech habits- helps adolescents develop critical thinking and emotional regulation skills in their online interactions. Studies have shown that adolescents whose parents engage in open, supportive communication about technology are more likely to use digital platforms responsibly and experience fewer negative emotional outcomes. Monitoring tools and parental controls, when used transparently and respectfully, can help create boundaries without compromising trust. However, excessive surveillance or punitive restrictions may backfire, leading to secrecy or resistance. Therefore, a balanced approach that combines structure with empathy is most effective. As digital life becomes increasingly central to adolescent development, parental guidance acts not just as a safeguard but also as a foundation for fostering digital literacy, resilience, and emotional well-being in a rapidly evolving online world.

The Effectiveness of Technology-Based Interventions in Supporting Adolescent Emotional Health

Technology-based interventions- such as online therapy platforms, mental health apps, and AI-driven Chabot's- have shown growing potential in supporting the emotional well-being of adolescents, particularly in contexts where traditional mental health services are limited, stigmatized, or inaccessible. Online therapy platforms like BetterHelp or Talkspace offer adolescents confidential access to licensed therapists, often at more flexible hours and lower costs, which appeals to young people seeking privacy or convenience. Mobile apps like Headspace, Calm, MindShift, and Woebot provide tools for mindfulness, mood tracking, cognitive behavioral therapy (CBT), and anxiety reduction—all accessible from a smartphone. Many adolescents report that these platforms help them manage stress, understand their emotions, and build healthier coping mechanisms.

Additionally, the anonymity and autonomy provided by such tools can empower teens who are hesitant to seek face-to-face therapy. However, the effectiveness of these interventions depends on several factors: the quality of the content, the user's level of engagement, and the presence of real-time human support when needed. Critics also caution against over-reliance on self-guided digital tools, as they may not be sufficient for complex or severe mental health conditions. Moreover, privacy concerns and the lack of regulation for some mental health apps remain significant barriers. In conclusion, while not a substitute for traditional therapy in all cases, technology-based interventions can be a valuable supplement or gateway to care- especially when thoughtfully integrated into a broader mental health support system tailored to adolescents' unique developmental needs.

Conclusion

In an era where digital technologies are deeply woven into the fabric of adolescent life, their impact on emotional health cannot be overlooked. While technology offers adolescents new avenues for connection, self-expression, and access to mental health resources, it also introduces challenges such as digital addiction, cyberbullying, and increased emotional vulnerability. Adolescents perceive both the benefits and limitations of online support systems—valuing their accessibility and anonymity, yet recognizing the risks of misinformation and emotional detachment. Technology-based interventions, including online therapy and mental health apps, show promising potential in addressing adolescent emotional needs, especially when used as complementary tools within a broader framework of care. However, the effectiveness of such interventions depends on their thoughtful design, ethical oversight, and the readiness of adolescents to engage meaningfully with them.

Equally crucial is the role of parental guidance and monitoring in shaping healthy digital habits and emotional resilience. When parents combine clear boundaries with open, empathetic communication, adolescents are more likely to navigate the digital world with awareness and emotional stability. Ultimately, supporting adolescent emotional health in the digital age requires a balanced and collaborative approach- one that integrates technological innovation, professional mental health support, informed parenting, and the active voices of adolescents themselves. Only then can we harness the power of technology not as a threat to emotional well-being, but as a meaningful ally in promoting psychological growth and resilience.

References

Boydell, K., Hodgins, M., Pignatiello, A., & Teshima, J. (2014).Using technology to deliver mental health services to children and youth: A scoping review. *Journal of the Canadian Academy of Child and Adolescent Psychiatry, 23*(2), 87–99

Callaghan, W. (2025, February 5). *Social media decoded: A guide for parents, grandparents, and teens to master strategies for online safety and digital literacy.*

Goldstein, M. A., & Goldstein, M. C. (2024, July 23). *How technology, social media, and current events profoundly affect adolescents.* Oxford University Press.

Jensen, M., George, M., Russell, M., & Odgers, C. (2019). Young adolescents' digital technology use and mental health symptoms: Little evidence of longitudinal or daily linkages. *Clinical Psychological Science, 7*(6), 1416–1433. https://doi.org/10.1177/2167702619859336

Odgers, C. L., & Jensen, M. (2020). Adolescent mental health in the digital age: Facts, fears, and future directions. *Journal of Child Psychology and Psychiatry, 61*(3), 336–348. https://doi.org/10.1111/jcpp.13190

Sagar, V. (2021, December 6). *Digital enlightenment: A book about internet addiction and ways to be focused in a digitally distracted world.* Notion Press.

Singh, A., Kumar, H., & Kumari, S. (2020). Impact of social media on adolescent's mental health, *8*(7).

Section II: Pedagogical Approaches and the Role of Teachers

7

The Future of Human Teachers in an AI-Powered World

Dr. Renuprava Sonowal

Assistant Professor, Department of Education
PDUA Mahavidyalaya, Dalgaon, Darrang, Assam
Email: renupravasonowal2802@gmail.com

Abstract

Traditional teaching and learning methods are changing as a result of artificial intelligence's (AI) quick advancement in the field of education. AI has created new opportunities for individualized and effective learning, from virtual assistants and intelligent tutoring systems to automated tests and predictive analytics. But this technology advancement also poses significant queries regarding the function of human educators in the future. While AI may handle data-driven jobs well, it lacks emotional intelligence, ethical reasoning, and the capacity to motivate and engage students on a human level. This paper examines the dynamic development of teaching roles in an AI-powered society. Instead, then replacing educators, the future of education will involve redefining their responsibilities as mentors, facilitators, and emotional support systems. By fusing the benefits of technology and human interaction, human-AI collaboration has the potential to improve educational outcomes. Prioritizing inclusive policies, ethical AI integration, and teacher training is necessary for this to succeed. According to the study's conclusions, human educators will continue to play a crucial role in education not because of artificial intelligence, but rather because of the indispensable human values they bring to the classroom in this increasingly digital day. Their changing role is essential in producing future students who are emotionally knowledgeable, well-rounded, and morally upright.

Keywords: *Artificial Intelligence, Education and Human Teachers,*

Introduction

Artificial intelligence (AI) has become a disruptive force in education in recent years, with advancements ranging from virtual assistants and automated grading tools to personalized learning platforms and intelligent tutoring systems. AI integration in education has never-before-seen benefits. Through adaptive learning algorithms, it supports a variety of learner demands, facilitates data-driven training, and lessens the administrative workload for teachers. In order to improve learning outcomes, AI-powered systems may analyse student performance in real-time, spot learning gaps, and offer tailored feedback. AI appears to be ready to take on a number of responsibilities that have historically been performed by educators. Both enthusiasm and worry have been raised by this development: joy about the improved accessibility and efficiency, as well as worry about the possible replacement of human teachers. But teaching involves more than just imparting knowledge and assigning grades. In addition to emotional intelligence, empathy, cultural awareness, and the capacity to mentor and inspire, it is a very human endeavour. Relationship development, identifying students' socio-emotional needs, and creating a welcoming and inclusive learning environment are all made possible by human teachers. Replicating these attributes is challenging, if not impossible, for AI. Teaching is about fostering critical thinking, creativity, moral reasoning, and personal development in addition to imparting knowledge. Furthermore, rather than doing away with the job of the teacher, the quick development of AI demands that it be redefined. Teachers will probably play more active and facilitating roles in an AI-enhanced classroom. They might develop into learning designers, helping pupils use digital resources and decipher insights produced by artificial intelligence. They must act as digital mentors, assisting students in developing digital literacy, challenging algorithmic prejudices, and becoming tech-savvy. Teachers could also be crucial in incorporating humanistic and ethical viewpoints into AI-powered education, making sure that technology is applied fairly and inclusively. Recognizing the disparity in access to AI technology and the digital gap across various socioeconomic categories and geographical areas is also crucial. In many regions of the world, especially in developing nations, the human teacher continues to be the cornerstone of the educational system. When infrastructure, digital literacy, and resource availability are still scarce, AI can help but cannot take their place. Human teachers will always be essential, even as AI continues to change the face of education. As technology advances, they will not be supplanted; rather, they will take on new tasks and responsibilities that combine the greatest aspects of human and machine talents. With AI as a potent tool in the hands of kind, knowledgeable, and flexible instructors, the future of education is probably going to be collaborative. The secret to creating an education system that is both highly technologically sophisticated and genuinely human-cantered is to embrace this synergy.

Capabilities of AI in Education

Artificial Intelligence (AI) is quickly changing the educational landscape by providing cutting-edge solutions that improve administrative, instructional, and learning effectiveness. Personalized learning is one of AI's primary educational applications, enabling systems to adjust pace and content to meet the needs of each unique student. AI-powered tools that can analyse students' strengths and shortcomings and provide tailored instruction include adaptive learning platforms and intelligent tutoring systems. **Holmes, W., Bialik, M., &Fadel, C. (2019)** Described how AI helps inclusive education by providing individualized learning routes, accessible tools, and multilingual content. Automated assessment and feedback is another important characteristic. AI allows for the immediate evaluation of tests and assignments, saving time and giving students rapid feedback. Additionally, by responding to questions, directing instruction, and monitoring progress, chatbots and virtual teaching assistants can help students around-the-clock. **Luckin, R. et al. (2016)** stressed that AI tools, such as intelligent tutoring, can improve individualized learning experiences by adjusting to students' needs and offering formative feedback. Another potent AI feature is predictive analytics, which enables teachers to spot at-risk pupils early and take appropriate action. **Chen, L., Chen, P., & Lin, Z. (2020)** Talked about how AI-based solutions offer real-time evaluation and feedback, promoting ongoing education and pointing out knowledge gaps. Additionally, AI promotes inclusive education by providing resources like language translation, speech-to-text, and customized content for students with disabilities or linguistic hurdles. **Baker, R. S., & Inventado, P. S. (2014)** Examined how AI can be used in predictive modelling to find kids who might need more academic help, which would increase retention and improve results. **Tuomi, I. (2018)** expressed that although AI can improve learning, its full potential can only be achieved when carefully combined with human direction and pedagogical objectives. Maintaining ethical use, data protection, and emotional support in educational environments requires striking a balance between AI and human involvement.

Evolving Role of Human Teachers

Human instructors' roles are changing from traditional knowledge transmitters to mentors, emotional advisors, and learning facilitators as Artificial Intelligence (AI) continues to transform education. Teachers are now concentrating more on helping students develop their critical thinking, creativity, emotional intelligence, and ethical reasoning skills because AI is taking care of repetitive chores like grading, lesson planning, and targeted material delivery. As they mentor students in group problem-solving and knowledge application in the real world, they are evolving into curators of valuable learning experiences. **Holmes et.al. (2019)** claimed that since AI cannot duplicate higher-order talents like creativity and ethics, educators will need to focus more on teaching them. Additionally, teachers are crucial in fostering welcoming and encouraging learning environments in the classroom something AI cannot do. Their capacity to comprehend the many needs of students reacts with empathy, and offer moral direction is still invaluable. Furthermore, human educators have a critical role in teaching student's media literacy, responsible technology use, and civic consciousness in an era of disinformation and digital distractions. **Luckin, R. et al. (2016)** highlight how educators may assist students understand AI-generated data and customize human support by acting as learning engineers. Teachers need continual professional development and digital literacy to succeed in this changing environment. Instead, then being replaced, educators are being repositioned as vital human pillars in a world of learning that is becoming more and more computerized.**Zawacki-Richter, O. et al. (2019)** emphasized that even while AI will help with teaching, human interaction is still essential for mentoring, inspiring, and providing moral guidance.

Human-AI Collaboration

Human-AI cooperation in education is a well-rounded strategy in which AI aids instruction while human teachers continue to play a crucial role in the educational process. **Rajasekar and Meenakshi (2020)** examined how AI tools might be used in Indian classrooms and underlined how crucial teacher-AI cooperation is to effective learning. They discovered that although AI can facilitate individualized instruction and expedite administrative duties, human educators are essential for deciphering AI-driven insights and fostering the moral and emotional growth of pupils. Their study also made clear the need for curriculum development and teacher training in order to foster productive human-AI collaboration in the classroom. Teachers may concentrate on student engagement, emotional support, and skill development by using AI tools to handle data-driven and repetitive chores like progress tracking, content delivery, and grading. This collaboration maintains the human touch necessary for social-emotional learning, ethical advice, and motivation while increasing efficiency and customisation. Teachers serve as facilitators in this type of paradigm, modifying their lessons to accommodate a range of learning demands by utilizing insights produced by AI. When people and AI work together effectively, technology will improve education rather than take the place of interpersonal relationships.

References

Baker, R. S., & Inventado, P. S. (2014).Educational data mining and learning analytics. In *Learning analytics* (pp. 61–75). Springer.

Chen, L., Chen, P., & Lin, Z. (2020). Artificial Intelligence in Education: A Review. *IEEE Access*, 8, 75264–75278.

Holmes, W., Bialik, M., & Fadel, C. (2019).*Artificial intelligence in education: Promises and implications for teaching and learning*. Centre for Curriculum Redesign.

Luckin, R., Holmes, W., Griffiths, M., & Forcier, L. B. (2016).*Intelligence Unleashed: An Argument for AI in Education*. Pearson Education.

Rajasekar, S., & Meenakshi, K. R. (2020). Human-AI Collaboration in Classrooms: A Study in Indian Educational Context. *International Journal of Educational Research and Technology*, 11

Tuomi, I. (2018). The impact of artificial intelligence on learning, teaching, and education. *European Commission JRC Science for Policy Report*.

8

The Role of Teachers in Supporting Student Mental Health

Dr. Mona Alice Marbaniang

Assistant Professor, Department of Social Work,
Girijananda Chowdhury University, Assam
Email: mona28marbz@gmail.com

Abstract

This paper highlights the critical role of teachers in supporting student mental health within school settings. Mental well-being is essential for children's overall development, yet academic pressure, competition, and lack of emotional support often lead to stress and isolation. Teachers, through daily interactions, are well-positioned to identify early signs of distress and offer timely support. However, challenges such as heavy workload, limited training, and emotional burnout hinder their efforts. The paper emphasizes the need for basic mental health training, structured emotional check-ins, and supportive school environments. Strengthening teacher capacity and well-being can significantly enhance students' emotional health, learning, and overall school experience.

Keywords: *Mental Health, Teachers & Well-Being*

Background

Mental health is a key part of a person's overall well-being. Without proper mental support and strength, it becomes difficult to function well in day-to-day life. The mind guides the body, and even when someone is physically healthy, if the mind is not at peace, they cannot truly feel well. Mental health has become a growing concern in today's world, and it holds importance in every stage of life.

In childhood, mental health is often shaped by the kind of family and background a child grows up in (Bornstein, 2013). As children grow older and begin spending more time outside the home, especially in school, their mental health starts being influenced by other factors such as friendships, school environment, teachers, peer pressure, and the wider community (Adkins, 2021). This is a crucial phase where strong emotional support can make a lasting difference. The kind of mental support received during these years plays a big role in shaping how emotionally strong and confident a person becomes in the future (McGorry & Mei, 2018). Therefore, it is important that the environment around growing children is healthy, positive, and encouraging.

A major part of childhood and adolescence is spent in school. Students meet their teachers and classmates every day, and the school environment becomes central to their learning and development. While parents guide and support children at home, teachers play a big role in shaping them during school hours (Jumatullailah et al., 2024). Since students come from different family backgrounds, not all of them receive the same kind of support at home. That is why it is important for teachers to also pay attention to students' mental well-being. Their care and understanding can shape a student's confidence, emotional balance, and self-worth (Zafar et al., 2025). Teachers are in a unique position to provide support, notice signs of distress, and help students feel safe and valued, not only in academics but in life as a whole.

Why Student Mental Health Needs Attention

Competition has always existed, but in today's world, it feels more intense than ever. This is seen not only among students but also among parents, who often push their children to perform better. There is constant pressure to come first, score high marks, and get into good colleges or universities. This pressure is not always openly talked about, but it builds up silently, creating stress that begins at a very young age. Students are expected to excel in every area such as academics, extracurricular activities, assignments, readings, and classwork (Pham, 2015). This overload can become overwhelming.

The stress to succeed can also lead to feelings of isolation and loneliness (Walsham et al., 2023). When students feel they can't keep up, they may start withdrawing from others, which affects their social life and emotional well-being. In some cases, extreme stress may even lead to behavioural issues, school dropout, or self-harm (Bhandari & Aryal, 2024; Ogresta et al., 2021; Raza et al., 2018). Apart from academic pressure, students also worry about their future, which adds to the anxiety.

All these challenges become harder to handle when there is a lack of emotional support and understanding from both families and the school system. Many schools are structured in a way that prioritizes results but overlooks mental well-being, making it even harder for students to cope. Emotional health directly affects focus, memory, and participation in class (Tyng et al., 2017). If mental health issues go unnoticed or untreated, they can lead to low self-esteem, poor performance, frequent absences, or dropping out of school (Nguyen et al 2019; Jones et al., 2009; Hjorth et al., 2016). Students may not always say what they are going through, but the signs often show up in their behaviour, mood, or performance. That is why this stage of life is so important, and why students need the right kind of support, especially from their teachers.

The Unique Role of Teachers

Teachers interact with students every day, which puts them in a unique position to notice sudden changes in mood or behaviour such as sadness, withdrawal, anger, or restlessness. These shifts might seem small at first, but they can often be early signs of emotional distress (Johnson et al., 2011). When teachers are attentive and caring, they have the opportunity to step in early and guide students toward the right kind of help. This support can be as simple as checking in with a student who seems upset, listening without judgment, or even offering a short break when someone looks overwhelmed. Being patient with students who are struggling to keep up with academics is also an important part of this support.

Harsh criticism or public scolding can sometimes worsen a student's emotional state (Oades-Sese et al., 2014). Instead, teachers can choose to encourage rather than punish, and create a space where students feel safe to express themselves. Building trust is key. When students feel they are treated with respect and kindness, they are more likely to open up about what they are going through. Encouraging peer support and open conversations within the classroom can also help reduce feelings of isolation among students (Carter et al., 2015).

Since teachers spend a significant amount of time with students, they often get to know their personalities, routines, and reactions. This puts them in a better position to notice when something is not right. Even though teachers may not be trained mental health professionals, they can still support student well-being through small yet impactful actions like practicing mindfulness exercises in class and promoting emotional regulation that take into account the past experiences and emotional needs of students (Meiklejohn et al., 2012).

If a student appears to be facing more serious challenges such as persistent stress, anxiety, or signs of depression, the teacher can help by referring them to the school counselor or connecting them with available mental health resources. In this way, teachers act as a bridge between students and the professional support systems they may need. By being observant, patient, and responsive, teachers play a vital role in promoting mental well-being in schools. Their everyday actions can make a lasting impact on how safe, understood, and supported students feel. This is why it is important that teachers are equipped to recognize emotional distress and take simple, practical steps to support mental health in their classrooms.

Challenges Teachers Face

While teachers play an important role in supporting students' mental health, it is also important to recognize the challenges they face in doing so. Teachers already carry a heavy workload, from preparing lesson plans, teaching multiple classes, conducting assessments, managing classroom behavior, to often taking on additional administrative or extracurricular responsibilities (Rajak& Chandra, 2017). With so much on their plate, it can be difficult to find the time or energy to give individual attention to students who may be struggling emotionally, especially in large classrooms where many students require support.

Another major challenge is that not all teachers are trained to recognize the signs of mental health issues in students. Spotting early warning signs like anxiety, depression, or trauma-related behavior is not always easy without proper training. Without this knowledge, even well-meaning teachers may feel unsure about how to respond or may unintentionally overlook students who need help (Andrews et al., 2014). Time constraints add to the difficulty. Teachers are often under pressure to complete the syllabus, conduct evaluations, and meet deadlines. This can make it hard to pause and have meaningful one-on-one interactions with students or to create space for mental health discussions in the classroom.

Teachers themselves can also experience emotional exhaustion or burnout. When they are overwhelmed or unsupported in their roles, it becomes even harder for them to provide emotional support to others (Arens & Morin, 2016). Their own mental well-being is just as important, and when neglected, it can limit their capacity to support their students effectively. Lastly, not all students feel comfortable opening up to teachers. There could be various reasons for this; fear of being judged, lack of trust, or past negative experiences. This makes it harder for teachers to know when a student is going through something difficult, even if they are willing to help.

These challenges highlight the need for a more supportive system where teachers are given the training, time, and emotional support they need to care for both their students' mental health and their own.

Recommendations

To make schools a better place for student mental health, there are a few simple but important steps that can be taken:

First, teachers should be given basic training in mental health awareness. They do not need to become full-time counselors, but some knowledge about common mental health issues, warning signs, and how to respond can really help (Jorm et al., 2010). When teachers know what to look for and how to react, they will feel more confident in supporting their students.

Second, schools can allow short mental health check-ins or sessions during class time (Esposito, 2025). It could be something as small as a five-minute talk about how students are feeling or a small mindfulness activity. These moments can really help students calm down, focus better, and feel cared for.

Third, schools should try to build a culture where it is okay to talk about emotions. Students should not feel embarrassed or scared to express when they are feeling stressed, anxious, or sad. Teachers and school staff can help by encouraging open conversations, being good listeners, and showing students that it is normal to talk about mental health.

In conclusion, while we focus on students, we should also remember that teachers need support too. Teaching can be stressful, and teachers also go through personal struggles. Schools should make sure that teachers have access to counseling services or at least a safe space to talk and take care of their own mental well-being. By making small changes like these, schools can become healthier spaces for both students and teachers, where mental health is taken seriously and everyone feels more supported.

Conclusion

Teachers are not trained therapists, and we should not expect them to be. But they are caring, observant, and deeply involved in the daily lives of students. This puts them in a powerful position to notice when something is not right and offer the first layer of support. With just a little training, encouragement, and school support, teachers can make a big difference in how students manage their mental health. When teachers feel supported and confident in this role, students benefit too. Because in the end, healthy students learn better, participate more, and feel more connected to school. So, if we want to truly support student mental health, we must start by supporting our teachers.

References

Adkins, I. (2021). Mental health and the impact of friendship. *WRIT: Journal of First-Year Writing, 4*(1), 4.

Andrews, A., McCabe, M., & Wideman-Johnston, T. (2014). Mental health issues in the schools: are educators prepared?.*The Journal of Mental Health Training, Education and Practice*, *9*(4), 261-272.

Arens, A. K., & Morin, A. J. (2016).Relations between teachers' emotional exhaustion and students' educational outcomes. *Journal of educational psychology*, *108*(6), 800.

Bornstein, M. H. (2013). Parenting and child mental health: a cross-cultural perspective. *World Psychiatry*, *12*(3), 258-265.

Esposito, G. (2025). Examining the Effects of a Tier 2 Check-in/Check-out Intervention on Middle School Aged Children: Check-ins and Logging Moods.

Hjorth, C. F., Bilgrav, L., Frandsen, L. S., Overgaard, C., Torp-Pedersen, C., Nielsen, B., & Bøggild, H. (2016). Mental health and school dropout across educational levels and genders: a 4.8-year follow-up study. *BMC public health*, *16*(1), 976.

Johnson, C., Eva, A. L., Johnson, L., & Walker, B. (2011). Don't turn away: Empowering teachers to support students' mental health. *The Clearing House: A Journal of Educational Strategies, Issues and Ideas*, *84*(1), 9-14.

Jones, R., Hoare, P., Elton, R., Dunhill, Z., & Sharpe, M. (2009). Frequent medical absences in secondary school students: survey and case–control study. *Archives of Disease in Childhood*, *94*(10), 763-767.

Jorm, A. F., Kitchener, B. A., Sawyer, M. G., Scales, H., &Cvetkovski, S. (2010). Mental health first aid training for high school teachers: a cluster randomized trial. *BMC psychiatry*, *10*(1), 51.

Jumatullailah, S. N., Maksum, A., &Nurhasanah, N. (2024). Literature Study: Analysis the Role of Teachers as Models in Strengthening Character in Primary School Learners. *At-Taqaddum*, *16*(2), 128-139.

McGorry, P. D., & Mei, C. (2018). Early intervention in youth mental health: progress and future directions. *BMJ Ment Health*, *21*(4), 182-184.

Meiklejohn, J., Phillips, C., Freedman, M. L., Griffin, M. L., Biegel, G., Roach, A., ...& Saltzman, A. (2012). Integrating mindfulness training into K-12 education: Fostering the resilience of teachers and students. *Mindfulness*, *3*(4), 291-307.

Nguyen, D. T., Wright, E. P., Dedding, C., Pham, T. T., & Bunders, J. (2019). Low self-esteem and its association with anxiety, depression, and suicidal ideation in Vietnamese secondary school students: a cross-sectional study. *Frontiers in psychiatry*, *10*, 438641.

Oades-Sese, G. V., Matthews, T. A., & Lewis, M. (2014).Shame and pride and their effects on student achievement. *International handbook of emotions in education*, 246-264.

Ogresta, J., Rezo, I., Kožljan, P., Paré, M. H., & Ajduković, M. (2021). Why do we drop out? Typology of dropping out of high school. *Youth & society*, *53*(6), 934-954.

Pham, T. T. B. (2015). *Study burden, academic stress and mental health among high school students in Vietnam* (Doctoral dissertation, Queensland University of Technology).

Rajak, R., & Chandra, B. (2017).Exploring predictors of burnout and work engagement among teachers-a review on higher educational institutions of India. *Journal of the Indian Academy of Applied Psychology*, *43*(1), 145.

Raza, A., Abbasi, N. U. H., Khurshid, M., & Ansari, M. I. (2018). The relationship between depression, anxiety, stress and self harm among college students: A cross-sectional survey. *Pakistan Armed Forces Medical Journal*, (1), 137-142.

Tyng, C. M., Amin, H. U., Saad, M. N., & Malik, A. S. (2017).The influences of emotion on learning and memory. *Frontiers in psychology*, *8*, 235933.

Walsham, W., Perlman, T. T., & Sihotang, D. (2023).Unraveling the threads: a comprehensive exploration of the interplay be-tween social isolation and academic stress among students. *Law and Economics*, *17*(3), 237-255.

Zafar, N., Butt, A. A., & Sardar, R. (2025). The Role of Teacher Attitudes in Shaping Students' Academic Confidence: A Survey-Based Study. *Journal of Religion and Society*, *4*(01), 249-263.

9

Fostering Resilience in Education: The Critical Role of Social Support Networks

Jhilam Gautam[1] & Dr. Tejoswita Gogoi[2]

Ph.D. Research Scholar[1]&Assistant Professor[2]
Department of Psychology, GirijanandaChowdhury University, Guwahati
Email: tejoswitagogoi@yahoo.com

Abstract

Mental health issues among students have become a pressing issue in school and university contexts. This chapter delves into the interrelated roles of social support, emotional resilience, and institutional interventions in influencing the well-being of students. Based on international research, considers the increasing incidence of ailments like anxiety, depression, and stress, and the disproportionate effect on marginalized student groups. Focus is given to the vital role of perceived social support from educators, peers, and family members in mitigating emotional and academic stressors. The chapter supports the inclusion of Social-Emotional Learning (SEL), mental health literacy, teacher training, and inclusive policies in the framework of education. In addition, it emphasizes the need for early detection of distress, reducing stigma, and cooperation between educators, psychologists, and policymakers. The implications are that resilience is not an innate characteristic but a context-dependent and teachable skill, developed in environments where emotional safety, inclusivity, and accessibility are paramount. In the end, the chapter requires education to adopt a systems and proactive stance towards mental health, with student well-being honored as the bedrock of academic achievement and lifelong personal growth.

Keywords: *Emotional resilience, social support, student well-being, Social Emotional Learning (SEL), stigma.*

Mental health challenges among students-whether in schools or universities are becoming increasingly widespread and serious. These issues are closely tied to three key factors: how easily students can access support, the stigma that still surrounds mental health, and the role of resilience in emotional well-being. A growing number of studies highlight just how common mental health struggles are in education. Conditions like depression, anxiety, suicidal thoughts, and stress-related disorders are showing up across all age groups. According to the World Health Organization (2021), around

10–20% of children and adolescents globally are affected by mental disorders-yet many go unnoticed and untreated. In universities, the picture is even more concerning, with about one in three college students experiencing a serious mental health issue during their studies (Auerbach et al., 2018). Many of these students report feeling isolated or discriminated against, which only worsens their symptoms and affects their ability to succeed academically (Eisenberg et al., 2009). However, there's encouraging evidence that resilience can be built. Programs that help students develop emotional regulation, flexible thinking, and strong social connections have been shown to reduce psychological distress (Connor & Davidson, 2003; Fergus & Zimmerman, 2005). That's why many schools are now including practices like mindfulness, peer support, emotional intelligence training, and problem-solving in their curriculum to help students better navigate the pressures of academic life (Durlak, 2011).

Rising Prevalence of Emotional Distress among Students

Traditionally, schools have responded to mental health challenges after they've become serious it's time for a shift. Mental health needs to be part of the proactive foundation of education. Promoting well-being, identifying early warning signs, and building resilience through the curriculum should be non-negotiables. Whole-school approaches that include teacher training, peer support, family involvement, and accessible counseling services have been proven to reduce emotional distress and boost student well-being (Weare, 2011).

Programs built around social-emotional learning (SEL), mindfulness, and cognitive-behavioral techniques can significantly ease anxiety and depression, while also helping students build emotional strength and self-control (Durlak, 2011). But for these efforts to work, schools must foster environments that are safe, inclusive, and free of judgment where students feel empowered to seek help without fear of stigma.

Reducing stigma must be an active part of any school mental health plan. That includes awareness campaigns, open conversations, and visible support systems. It also means ensuring that all students-especially those from marginalized backgrounds, such as minority communities, LGBTQ+ students, and those facing financial hardship-have fair and equal accesses to mental health care.

Investing in these systems doesn't just lead to better mental health outcomes. It also supports academic success, improves attendance, and helps keep students engaged (Kern, Waters, Adler, & White, 2017). In the long run, these strategies nurture emotionally intelligent, resilient, and socially aware individuals that are essential far beyond the classroom.

Social Support in Shaping Student Outcomes

Support from others-whether it's family, friends, teachers, or the broader school system-plays a powerful role in protecting students' mental health. Both the perception and the reality of having help available can make a big difference. Social support strengthens emotional resilience, promotes healthier ways of coping, and acts as a cushion against academic stress and social challenges (Zimet, Dahlem, Zimet, & Farley, 1988). On the flip side, when students don't feel supported when support systems are lacking-they're more vulnerable to emotional instability and mental health struggles, especially during stressful transitions or setbacks.

This chapter explores how different forms of support influence students' mental health together and on their own. The goal is to offer insights that can inform the creation of safe, supportive, and stigma-free classrooms that not only address mental health issues but also actively nurture resilience and emotional well-being.

Mental Health in the Educational Context

Mental health is more than just the absence of illness- it's about feeling well enough to handle life's challenges, recognize your strengths, learn and work effectively, and contribute to the world around you (World Health Organization (WHO) Suicide: Key facts., 2021). It's a complex blend of emotional, psychological, and social well-being that influences how we think, feel, behave, manage stress, relate to others, and make everyday decisions.

A key part of this is emotional resilience, the ability to adapt during tough times. According to the American Psychological Association (2020), resilient individuals "roll with the punches," bouncing back from stress or crisis without long-term difficulty. Resilience isn't about avoiding hardship- it's about recovering from it. It's built on psychological flexibility, emotional regulation, and healthy coping habits.

Emerging Mental Health Trends among Youth

Recent research highlights some concerning trends:

- **Mental Health on the Rise**: The Lancet Commission estimates that by 2030, nearly a billion young people could face preventable mental health challenges like depression and anxiety (Half a billion young people will be obese or overweight by 2030, report finds, 2025)
- **The COVID-19 Effect**: The pandemic worsened the situation. Symptoms of depression and anxiety among youth doubled during this period.
- **Socioeconomic Inequality**: A long-term study (2004–2020) found that mental health has improved for adolescents from higher socioeconomic backgrounds, while it has either stagnated or worsened for those from lower-income families to widening mental health disparities.
- **Gender Gaps**: The same study revealed a decline in depression and suicidal thoughts among girls, but not among boys, suggesting that mental health interventions may need to be more gender-sensitive.
- **Academic Pressure**: Unsurprisingly, high academic demands are closely linked to higher rates of depression and anxiety among students.

- **The Need for Targeted Support**: Experts recommend tailored support offering clear pathways to help and focusing on students who are most at risk, instead of relying on generic programs that try to cover everyone.
- **The Social Media Double-Edged Sword:** On one hand, heavy social media use has been tied to increased loneliness, anxiety, and depression among teens. On the other, digital tools like mental health apps and AI chatbots - when thoughtfully designed - can offer accessible support, especially if they respect cultural and privacy concerns.

Challenges to Mental Health in Educational Systems

Academic Stress

For many adolescents, school is a major source of pressure. The constant push to excel- be it through grades, exams, or competition takes a serious toll on mental health. Research shows that when students feel overwhelmed by academic expectations, they're more likely to experience symptoms of anxiety and depression.

Peer Pressure

The desire to fit in is especially strong during adolescence - some students feel they have to go along with the crowd, which can sometimes mean engaging in risky behavior like substance use or adopting unhealthy coping mechanisms. This kind of pressure often chips away at self-esteem and can lead to emotional distress.

Digital Influences

Technology has transformed the way students learn and connect but it's not without downsides. Too much time on social media can lead to comparison, feelings of inadequacy, loneliness, and even cyberbullying. Long-term studies have found that overuse of social platforms is linked to increased depression and lower life satisfaction in teens.

Identity Formation

Adolescence is a time of self-discovery. But this journey of figuring out "who I am" can be easily thrown off course by negative online comparisons, cultural stigma, or rejection from peers. When identity development is disrupted, it often leads to confusion, low self-worth, and mental strain. Research connects these experiences with higher levels of anxiety and depression.

Institutional Neglect

Students don't just need academic instruction-they need emotional support, too. Unfortunately, many schools are under-resourced, lack trained mental health professionals, or rely on punitive approaches to discipline. When students feel unseen or unsupported, their emotional health suffers. Evidence shows that having trained school-based mental health staff makes a real difference in reducing student distress-but too many schools are still missing this critical support.

Perceived Social Support

Perceived social support is all about the belief that you're not alone there are people in your life who care about you, value you, and are there to help when you need it. Whether it's family, friends, or trusted adults, this sense of connection plays a powerful role in how we handle stress. As Cobb (1976) put it, it's the feeling of being part of a network that offers emotional and practical support to help us cope with life's challenges (Cobb, 1976).

How Support Makes a Difference

1. **It makes stress feel more manageable**: Just knowing you have someone to lean on can make tough situations feel less threatening.
2. **It strengthens coping skills**: Supportive relationships often encourage healthy ways of dealing with problems talking things through or finding practical solutions.
3. **It offers emotional relief**: Being able to share your worries with someone you trust can ease feelings of loneliness, anxiety, or sadness.
4. **It supports physical health, too**: Believe it or not, strong social connections can actually lower stress hormones like cortisol and even boost your immune system.

Educational Strategies to Foster Supportive Environments

1. Bring in Social and Emotional Learning (SEL) Programs

SEL helps students build essential life skills understanding their emotions, showing empathy, making thoughtful decisions, and forming healthy relationships. These programs don't just boost emotional well-being; they improve behavior and academic performance too. A large-scale analysis of 213 studies found that students in SEL programs showed clear gains in social skills, attitudes, and academic success compared to their peers.

Students who have family members with physical diseases such as cancer, or who are survivors themselves, often face emotional challenges that go unnoticed in school settings. Studies have shown that adolescents who experience chronic illness or live with ill relatives report higher levels of stress, anxiety, and depressive symptoms (Thompson, Gustafson, Hamlett, & Spock, 2009). Without the right support or understanding from peers and educators, this emotional weight can affect learning, relationships, and well-being.

Moreover, there is growing recognition that resilience is not a fixed trait, but a skill that can be taught and nurtured - especially in schools (Masten, 2018). When students are equipped with the tools to understand, process, and support others through health-related challenges like cancer, they become more emotionally prepared to handle adversity.

When schools combine mental health literacy with education about real-world physical health challenges like cancer, they help students holistically understand health. It's not just about treating illness- it's about recognizing the role of support, self-awareness, and resilience in recovery and everyday life. This approach reflects what research and lived experience continues to show: that no one faces illness in isolation, and healing is just as much about the heart and mind as it is about the body.

2. Strengthen Teacher-Student Relationships

When students feel seen and supported by their teachers, everything changes. Encouraging educators to build strong, trusting relationships with students can lower rates of depression, boost engagement, and increase motivation. Positive teacher-student connections also help buffer emotional stress and create a healthier, more inclusive school climate.

3. Foster Inclusive and Safe School Environments

Creating a school culture that values diversity, equity, and inclusion (DEI) is crucial. This means enforcing anti-bullying policies, offering gender sensitivity training, and celebrating cultural differences. When students feel accepted and safe, especially those from marginalized backgrounds, they're more likely to thrive emotionally and academically.

4. Teach Mental Health Literacy

By making mental health part of the regular curriculum, schools can normalize conversations around well-being. Teaching students about mental health, self-care, stigma, and how to seek help empowers them to take care of themselves and others. Programs like *The Mental Health and High School Curriculum Guide* have been shown to increase awareness and improve attitudes toward mental health.

5. Ensure Access to Counseling and Peer Support

Every student should have easy access to trained counselors and peer support networks. On-campus mental health professionals and structured peer groups provide a safe, approachable space for students to talk and get help. Early intervention through these supports can significantly reduce symptoms of anxiety, depression, and even suicidal thoughts.

6. Identifying Early Warning Signs

In a supportive school environment, one of the most powerful things we can do is catch mental health struggles early and create space for hope. Early identification and prevention are key to helping students stay emotionally well and succeed long-term.

7. Recognizing the Early Warning Signs

Emotional distress often starts subtly-things like pulling away from others, losing interest in school, becoming irritable, sleeping poorly, struggling to focus, or a noticeable drop in academic performance. These signs often come before more serious mental health conditions like depression, anxiety, or suicidal thoughts (Bor et al., 2014).

Unfortunately, in schools where mental health isn't openly discussed, these behaviors might be mistaken for laziness or bad behavior. That's why it's so important to train teachers, school staff, and even students to recognize these early red flags. When the school community knows what to look for and how to respond, it opens the door for early support. Research shows that early detection and timely referrals can ease emotional distress and even boost academic performance (Loades & Mastroyannopoulou, 2010).

Tackling Stigma and Promoting a Culture of Support

To truly support student mental health, schools need a broad, multi-layered strategy that tackles stigma on every level-system-wide, socially, and individually.

Anti-Stigma Campaigns

Mental health literacy campaigns that share personal stories, spotlight peer advocates, and focus on fact-based education can significantly shift attitudes. These efforts help normalize seeking help and reduce the shame often tied to mental health issues (Thornicroft et al., 2016).

Open Dialogue and Peer Support

Creating spaces for classroom discussions, workshops, and school forums where students can talk openly about mental health is essential. When teachers use inclusive language and when peer support is available, it builds a culture of trust and openness (Naslund et al., 2017).

Policy and Institutional Changes

Schools must back these cultural shifts with strong policies. That includes offering confidential and easily accessible counseling services, ensuring that seeking help never affects academic standing, making mental health orientation part of student and staff onboarding, weaving mental health topics into the curriculum, and having clear protocols for crises.

Emotional Resilience as a Protective Factor

Emotional resilience is what helps people stay steady or bounce back when life gets tough. Scholars define it as "the capacity to maintain or regain psychological well-being in the face of challenge" (Herrman, et al., 2011). In school or university settings, this resilience is especially important. It's about how students, researchers, and educators handle the ups and downs of academic life like bad grades, high expectations, constant competition, or the pressure to perform (Turner, 2017). Resilience doesn't mean avoiding stress altogether means facing challenges head-on, learning from them, and continuing to move forward with purpose and hope.

How Can Schools Help Build Resilience?

One of the most effective ways is through Social Emotional Learning (SEL) which was discussed earlier in this chapter. When students learn to manage their feelings, connect with others, and respond constructively to setbacks, they're better equipped to handle stress and thrive under pressure.

Another powerful approach is mindfulness. When students are taught to focus on the present moment with openness and without judgment, it can ease anxiety, improve focus, and help with emotional regulation. These benefits are especially helpful in high-stakes academic settings. A meta-analysis by Zenner, Herrnleben-Kurz, and Walach (2014) found that mindfulness programs in schools significantly improved students' emotional and cognitive functioning (Zenner et al., 2014).

Life skills education rounds out the toolkit. These are practical, everyday skills like problem-solving, critical thinking, effective communication, and stress management. According to the World Health Organization (1997), these skills are essential for handling life's demands. When students develop these abilities, they become more confident and adaptable, better prepared to face challenges, and more likely to make balanced, thoughtful decisions.

The Role of Institutional Policies and Educator Training in Cultivating Resilience

Institutional policies lay the groundwork for creating a learning environment where emotional resilience can truly take root. When schools and universities commit to policies that put student well-being, inclusion, and mental health at the forefront, they help build a culture where students can learn to cope, adapt, and thrive. For instance, embedding Social Emotional Learning (SEL) into the curriculum, ensuring access to mental health support, and actively preventing bullying are all proven ways to strengthen resilience and improve academic outcomes (Taylor et al., 2017).

Just as important is making sure educators have the tools they need. When teachers and school staff are trained in SEL, trauma-informed care, and culturally responsive teaching, they're better prepared to create emotionally safe, supportive, and engaging classrooms (Jennings et al., 2011). With the right training, they can also spot early signs of emotional distress and know how to step in or refer students to the right support-creating a more responsive and compassionate school environment (Brunzell et al., 2016).

Policy and educator training works best when they're in sync. Policies provide the structure, while trained educators bring those values to life every day. When both are aligned, schools become spaces where students and staff are empowered to face challenges with confidence, flexibility, and a sense of purpose.

Recommendations

In today's fast-paced and high-pressure academic world, emotional resilience isn't just a nice-to-have-it's essential. For both students and educators, the ability to handle stress, bounce back from setbacks, and protect their mental well-being plays a huge role in academic success and long-term personal and professional growth.

But resilience doesn't grow on its own. It's shaped by a mix of personal traits, supportive learning environments, and strong public policies. That's why building emotionally resilient school communities requires action on multiple levels students, schools, and policymakers. The following recommendations outline what each group can do to create lasting, supportive systems where everyone has the tools they need to thrive.

For Schools and Universities: Creating Resilient Learning Environments

Educational institutions play a critical role in shaping the culture students experience every day. To promote resilience:

a. ***Embed SEL and Life Skills into the Curriculum***: Teach these skills early and often so students can apply them when it counts (Taylor et al., 2017).

b. ***Invest in Educator Training***: Equip teachers and staff with the knowledge and tools to foster emotional safety and spot signs of distress (Jennings et al., 2011).

c. ***Build Safe and Inclusive Campuses***: Celebrate diversity, enforce anti-bullying practices, and make sure every student feels they belong.

d. ***Improve Access to Mental Health Services***: Ensure students can easily find professional help on campus when they need it.

e. ***Promote a Healthy Academic Culture***: Encourage balance, recognize effort over perfection, and create space for students to recharge.

Encouraging Interdisciplinary Collaboration between Educators, Psychologists, and Policymakers

Promoting emotional resilience and mental well-being in schools and universities isn't something any one group can do alone. It takes a coordinated, collaborative effort that brings together educators, psychologists, and policymakers. When these groups work in sync, they can design and implement strategies that not only support individual student needs but also address wider, system-level challenges.

Teachers are often the first to notice when a student is struggling emotionally. But without proper training, they may not feel equipped to offer the right kind of support. That's where psychologists come bringing valuable expertise in assessment, intervention, and the design of evidence-based mental health programs (Weare, 2015). Policymakers play a different but equally vital role. Through legislation, funding, and policy-making, they help scale successful initiatives and make sure effective mental health programs aren't just temporary projects but long-term, embedded parts of the education system (Barry et al., 2013).

To make this collaboration work, we need structures that connect these groups to joint advisory boards, cross-sector working groups, and inclusive policy-making that listens to all voices involved. When educators, psychologists, and policymakers share ownership and responsibility, they can build a more unified, compassionate, and effective mental health strategy for schools. It's this kind of partnership that turns good ideas into lasting change.

Conclusion

As educational institutions grapple with rising mental health challenges among students, this chapter underscores the urgent need to adopt a proactive, inclusive, and multi-layered approach to psychological well-being in academic settings. Mental health is not merely an individual concern but a collective responsibility shaped profoundly by the presence or absence of social support, institutional structures, and stigma reduction initiatives.

The evidence presented illustrates that resilience is not an inherent trait but a learnable skill that thrives in environments where students feel seen, supported, and safe. By integrating social-emotional learning, mental health literacy, supportive educator relationships, and targeted interventions into educational systems, we can equip students with the tools necessary to navigate adversity and thrive both academically and emotionally.

Ultimately, fostering mental well-being in education requires sustained commitment and collaboration between students, educators, psychologists, and policymakers. Together, they can cultivate a culture that not only mitigates mental distress but actively builds resilience, reduces stigma, and prepares young minds to flourish in an increasingly complex world. Education, at its best, must nurture the whole individual intellectually, emotionally, and socially.

References

Auerbach, R. P., Mortier, P., & Bruffaerts, R. (2018). WHO World Mental Health Surveys International College Student Project: Prevalence and distribution of mental disorders. *Journal of Abnormal Psychology, 127*(7), 623-638. doi:https://doi.org/10.1037/a

Bor, W., Dean, A. J., Najman, J., & Hayatbakhsh, R. (2014). Are child and adolescent mental health problems increasing in the 21st century? A systematic review. *Australian & New Zealand Journal of Psychiatry, 48*(7), 606-616. doi:https://doi.org/10.1177/000

Cobb, S. (1976). Social support as a moderator of life stress. Psychosomatic Medicine.*38*(5), 300–314. doi:https://doi.org/10.1097/00006842-197609000-00003

Durlak, J. A. (2011). The impact of enhancing students' social and emotional learning: A meta-analysis of school-based universal interventions. *Child Development, 82*(1), 405-432. doi: https://doi.org/10.1111/j.1467-86

Eisenberg, D., Hunt, J., &Speer, N. (2009). Mental health in American colleges and universities: Variation across student subgroups and campuses. *The Journal of Nervous and Mental Disease, 197*(1), 60-67. doi: https://doi.org/10.1097/NMD.0b013e3181924d2

Fergus, S., & Zimmerman, M. A. (2005). Adolescent resilience: A framework for understanding healthy development in the face of risk. *Annual Review of Public Health*, 399–419. doi: https://doi.org/10.1146/annurev.publhealth.26.021304.144357

Herrman, H., Stewart, D. E., Diaz-Granados, N., Berger, E. L., Jackson, B., & Yuen, T. (2011). What is resilience? *The Canadian Journal of Psychiatry, 56*(5), 258-265. doi:https://doi.org/10.1177/070674371105600504

Kern, M. L., Waters, L. E., Adler, A., & White, M. A. (2017).Assessing employee wellbeing in schools using a multifaceted approach: Associations with physical health, life satisfaction, and professional thriving. *Psychology, 6*, 978–996.

Loades, M. E., & Mastroyannopoulou, K. (2010).Teachers' recognition of children's mental health problems.*Child and Adolescent Mental Health, 15*(3), 150–156. . doi:https://doi.org/10.1111/j.1475-3588.2009.00551.x

Masten, A. S. (2018). Resilience in children: Developmental perspectives. *Children, 5*(7), 98.doi:https://doi.org/10.3390/children5070098

Naslund, J. A., Aschbrenner, K. A., Marsch, L. A., & Bartels, S. J. (2017). The future of mental health care: Peer-to-peer support and social media. *Epidemiology and Psychiatric Sciences, 25*(5), 113-122. doi:https://doi.org/10.1017/S2045796015001067

Thompson, R. J., Gustafson, K. E., Hamlett, K. W., & Spock, A. (2009). Psychological adjustment of children with cystic fibrosis: The role of child cognitive processes and maternal adjustment. *Journal of Pediatric Psychology, 17*(6), 741-755.

Thornicroft, G., Mehta, N., & Clement, S. (2016). Evidence for effective interventions to reduce mental-health-related stigma and discrimination.*The Lancet*, 1123–1132. doi: https://doi.org/10.1016/S0140-6736(15)00298-6

Turner, M. H.-Y. (2017). Resilience at university: The development and testing of a new measure. *Higher Education Research & Development, 36*(2), 386–400. . doi:https://doi.org/10.1080/07294360.2016.1185398

Weare, K. &. (2011). Mental health promotion and problem prevention in schools: What does the evidence say? *Health Promotion International*, 129-169. doi:https://doi.org/10.1093/heapro/dar075

Zenner, C., Herrnleben-Kurz, S., & Walach, H. (2014).Mindfulness-based interventions in schools—a systematic review and meta-analysis.*Frontiers in Psychology*, 603. doi:https://doi.org/10.3389/fpsyg.2014.00603

Zimet, G. D., Dahlem, N. W., Zimet, S. G., & Farley, G. K. (1988). The Multidimensional Scale of Perceived Social Support. *Journal of Personality Assessment, 52*(1), 30-41. doi: https://doi.org/10.1207/s15327752jpa5201_2

10

The Synergy of Eastern and Western Approaches: Exploring the Integration of Mindfulness Practices into Cognitive Behavioral Frameworks

Kongkana Pathak

Research Scholar, Department of Education,
Mahapurusha Srimanta Sankaradeva Viswavidyalaya, Nagaon
Email: kongkanapathak879@gmail.com

Abstract

The growing prevalence of stress, anxiety, and depression has prompted mental health professionals to explore more holistic and integrative therapeutic models. This paper examines the synergy between Eastern contemplative practices, particularly mindfulness and meditation and Western psychological approaches, with a specific focus on their integration within Cognitive Behavioral Therapy (CBT). Drawing on both theoretical frameworks and empirical studies, the paper explores how mindfulness practices, rooted in Buddhist traditions, complement CBT's structured and goal-oriented methods by enhancing clients' awareness of automatic thoughts, emotional regulation, and present-moment engagement. The study also analyses Mindfulness-Based Cognitive Therapy (MBCT) and Acceptance and Commitment Therapy (ACT) as leading examples of this integration. It concludes by highlighting the benefits, limitations, and practical implications of integrating Eastern mindfulness with Western cognitive models, suggesting that such cross-cultural therapeutic paradigms offer a more person-centered and adaptable approach to mental health care in a globalized world.

Keywords: *Cognitive Behavioral Therapy, Acceptance and Commitment Therapy, Mindful practices, Eastern and Western Philosophy*

Introduction

In recent decades, mental health treatment has witnessed a transformative shift toward more integrative and holistic approaches. While Western psychology has long emphasized cognitive restructuring, behavioral modification, and evidence-based practices, Eastern philosophies particularly those rooted in Buddhism, such as mindfulness and meditation, offer complementary tools that address the experiential and existential aspects of human suffering. Among Western modalities, Cognitive Behavioral Therapy (CBT) has emerged as one of the most widely researched and applied psychotherapeutic frameworks for treating anxiety, depression, and a range of stress-related disorders. However, its traditional focus on cognitive distortions and behavioral change can sometimes overlook the value of present-moment awareness, emotional acceptance, and non-judgmental observation—core tenets of mindfulness-based practices.

The increasing interest in bridging these paradigms has given rise to integrative models such as Mindfulness-Based Cognitive Therapy (MBCT) and Acceptance and Commitment Therapy (ACT), which embed Eastern mindfulness techniques within the structured, goal-oriented scaffolding of CBT. These models aim not only to reduce psychological symptoms but also to enhance overall well-being, resilience, and emotional regulation. This integration reflects a broader movement in global mental health that seeks to combine the analytical strengths of Western science with the introspective wisdom of Eastern traditions.

This paper explores the theoretical and practical convergence between mindfulness and CBT, examining how their integration contributes to more comprehensive and adaptive therapeutic outcomes. By reviewing current literature, case studies, and empirical findings, the study aims to evaluate the effectiveness of such hybrid approaches and their implications for contemporary mental health practice. In doing so, it underscores the potential of cross-cultural synthesis in shaping the future of psychotherapy.

Mindfulness in Eastern Philosophy and Western Psychology

Mindfulness, though widely discussed in contemporary psychology, finds its origins in ancient Eastern spiritual and philosophical traditions, particularly within Buddhism. In Pāli, the term sati (translated as "mindfulness") is a central component of the Noble Eightfold Path in Buddhist teachings, which emphasizes right awareness as essential to overcoming suffering (dukkha) (Kabat-Zinn, 2003). In this traditional context, mindfulness is not merely a technique, but a way of being rooted in ethical conduct, wisdom, and meditative discipline.

A classic example of mindfulness in Buddhist practice is Vipassana meditation, which involves focused attention on the breath and bodily sensations while maintaining non-judgmental awareness of thoughts and emotions. This practice is designed to foster insight into the nature of the self and reality, ultimately leading to liberation from suffering. The meditative process cultivates equanimity, detachment, and a profound understanding of impermanence (anicca), non-self (anattā), and suffering (dukkha).

The Western adaptation of mindfulness began in earnest with Jon Kabat-Zinn, who secularized these principles into the Mindfulness-Based Stress Reduction (MBSR) program in the late 1970s. Kabat-Zinn (1990) defined mindfulness as "paying attention in a particular way: on purpose, in the present moment, and nonjudgmentally." MBSR was originally developed for patients with chronic pain but has since been applied to a wide range of psychological and medical conditions. The program retains core

Buddhist elements such as breath awareness, body scan meditation, and mindful movement (e.g., yoga), but reframes them in secular, therapeutic language.

Western psychology has embraced mindfulness as a powerful tool for enhancing emotional regulation, reducing rumination, and increasing psychological flexibility. For example, in Dialectical Behavior Therapy (DBT), developed by Marsha Linehan, mindfulness is one of the core skills taught to clients struggling with borderline personality disorder (Linehan, 1993). It helps clients become more aware of their thoughts and urges without immediately reacting, thus improving impulse control and emotional regulation.

Another notable integration is seen in Mindfulness-Based Cognitive Therapy (MBCT), where mindfulness is used to help individuals recognize negative thought patterns before they escalate into depressive episodes. In a seminal randomized controlled trial, Teasdale et al. (2000) found that MBCT significantly reduced relapse rates in patients with recurrent depression compared to treatment as usual.

Furthermore, neuroimaging studies have provided empirical support for the efficacy of mindfulness practices. Research by Holzel et al. (2011) revealed that participants in an 8-week MBSR program exhibited increased gray matter density in brain regions associated with learning, memory, emotion regulation, and self-referential processing.

Thus, while Eastern traditions view mindfulness as part of a broader spiritual path, Western psychology has adapted it as a therapeutic technique. Despite differences in underlying metaphysics and goals, both traditions converge in recognizing the value of mindful awareness in transforming human experience and alleviating suffering.

Bridging Traditions: The Emergence of Integrative Therapies

The integration of Eastern contemplative practices with Western psychological models has given rise to a new wave of integrative therapies and frameworks that harness the strengths of both traditions to address mental health holistically. Among these, the synthesis of mindfulness with Cognitive Behavioral Therapy (CBT) represents one of the most significant developments in contemporary psychotherapy.

Cognitive Behavioral Therapy (CBT), developed in the 1960s by Aaron Beck, is grounded in the idea that maladaptive thoughts influence emotions and behaviors (Beck, 1976). CBT aims to identify and restructure distorted thought patterns, such as catastrophizing or black-and-white thinking, to foster healthier emotional responses. The therapy is structured, time-limited, and problem-focused making it one of the most empirically validated treatments for disorders like depression, anxiety, and PTSD (Butler et al., 2006).

However, traditional CBT has faced criticism for its emphasis on cognitive change and symptom reduction, often overlooking deeper existential concerns or the acceptance of internal experiences. This gap has been addressed by therapies that incorporate mindfulness and acceptance, such as Acceptance and Commitment Therapy (ACT).

ACT, developed by Steven C. Hayes and colleagues in the 1980s, belongs to the "third wave" of behavioral therapies. Unlike traditional CBT, which focuses on changing negative thoughts, ACT teaches clients to accept their thoughts and emotions without judgment and to commit to actions aligned with their core values (Hayes, Strosahl, & Wilson, 1999). It promotes psychological flexibility, which is defined as the ability to stay in contact with the present moment while behaving in ways consistent with one's chosen values even in the face of difficult thoughts and feelings.

Similarly, Mindfulness-Based Cognitive Therapy (MBCT), developed by Segal, Williams, and Teasdale (2002), integrates mindfulness practices with core CBT techniques. Initially designed to prevent relapse in individuals with recurrent depression, MBCT helps clients become aware of early signs of depressive thinking and respond with mindful awareness rather than automatic rumination. In an MBCT session, clients may practice body scans, sitting meditations, and mindful movement, followed by discussions on how these practices relate to their thoughts and moods. This blend of present-moment awareness and cognitive reflection bridges the theoretical frameworks of both East and West.

Empirical research supports the efficacy of these integrative approaches. A meta-analysis by Hofmann et al. (2010) found that mindfulness-based therapies are highly effective in reducing anxiety and depression. Similarly, ACT has demonstrated effectiveness across a range of clinical conditions, including chronic pain, substance abuse, and PTSD (A-Tjak et al., 2015).

These integrative models do more than combine techniques; they reflect a philosophical shift in how mental health is understood. By uniting the Eastern emphasis on acceptance and awareness with the Western focus on structured intervention and cognitive clarity, therapies like ACT and MBCT offer a more nuanced, person-centered approach to psychological healing.

The Role of Meditation in Cognitive and Acceptance-Based Therapies

Meditation, particularly in the form of mindfulness-based practices has emerged as a powerful intervention in managing stress and anxiety within both Cognitive Behavioral Therapy (CBT) and Acceptance and Commitment Therapy (ACT). While these two therapeutic models differ in their approaches to cognition and behaviour, both now incorporate meditation techniques to foster mental clarity, emotional regulation, and non-reactive awareness. Rather than attempting to eliminate distressing thoughts or emotions, meditation within these therapies aims to change the individual's relationship to internal experiences, enabling healthier coping responses.

Meditation within Cognitive Behavioral Therapy

In recent years, CBT has evolved beyond its original focus on cognitive restructuring to include experiential techniques such as mindfulness meditation. These practices are used to help clients increase awareness of automatic thoughts without being overwhelmed or immediately reacting to them. For example, in cases of generalized anxiety disorder, a mindfulness-based CBT program may involve a "thought watching" meditation, where clients are guided to sit quietly and note thoughts as they arise, labeling them without attachment (e.g., "worrying," "planning," "judging").

This process helps disrupt habitual patterns of rumination and catastrophizing by reinforcing a neutral, observational stance. Research by Evans et al. (2008) found that a group-based mindfulness CBT intervention led to significant reductions in anxiety and perceived stress, particularly among patients with persistent worry and somatic symptoms.

Another study by Hofmann, Sawyer, and Fang (2010) reported that integrating mindfulness into CBT enhances meta-cognitive awareness, which allows individuals to view their thoughts as transient rather than defining truths—an essential step in breaking the cycle of stress-induced thinking.

Meditation within Acceptance and Commitment Therapy

In ACT, meditation is embedded in the core processes of therapy, serving not only as a technique for relaxation but also as a gateway to acceptance, defusion, and value-driven action. ACT often uses brief, guided meditative exercises such as "Leaves on a Stream", where clients imagine placing each thought on a leaf and watching it float away. This meditative imagery helps reduce the believability and impact of negative thoughts, reinforcing ACT's principle of cognitive defusion.

A randomized controlled trial by Forman et al. (2007) demonstrated that ACT participants showed greater improvements in emotional acceptance and reduced experiential avoidance, leading to lower stress and anxiety levels, compared to traditional CBT participants who focused solely on thought restructuring.

Additionally, meditation in ACT supports values clarification—for instance, during a quiet reflection exercise, clients might meditate on what truly matters to them, anchoring their future actions not in avoidance of stress, but in pursuit of meaningful life directions.

Broader Therapeutic Implications

Both CBT and ACT use meditation to shift the therapeutic goal from merely "feeling better" to "functioning better with one's feelings." While CBT uses mindfulness to help clients recognize and interrupt distorted thinking patterns, ACT employs meditation to foster acceptance and committed action in the presence of discomfort. In both cases, meditation cultivates present-moment awareness, which has been linked to improved emotional regulation, decreased physiological arousal, and enhanced overall psychological resilience.

Conclusion

The integration of Eastern contemplative practices particularly mindfulness and meditation with Western psychotherapeutic models such as Cognitive Behavioral

Therapy (CBT) and Acceptance and Commitment Therapy (ACT) marks a significant evolution in the landscape of mental health care. While CBT traditionally emphasizes cognitive restructuring and behavioral interventions, and ACT promotes acceptance and value-driven action, both approaches increasingly recognize the transformative potential of mindfulness and meditative awareness in managing stress, anxiety, and emotional dysregulation.

Mindfulness, rooted in Buddhist philosophy, offers more than a technique. It offers a paradigm shift that encourages individuals to observe their thoughts and emotions without judgment. When embedded into CBT and ACT, meditation helps clients relate differently to distressing thoughts, reduce rumination, and cultivate emotional resilience. Empirical studies affirm that these integrative models not only reduce symptoms but also foster psychological flexibility, self-awareness, and long-term well-being.

As mental health challenges become more complex and culturally diverse, these cross-traditional therapeutic frameworks offer a more holistic, adaptive, and person-centered approach. They move beyond symptom management to empower individuals to live with greater presence, clarity, and purpose. In doing so, the synthesis of Eastern and Western healing paradigms contributes meaningfully to the future of global mental health practice—one that honours both scientific rigor and contemplative wisdom.

References

A-Tjak, J. G. L., Davis, M. L., Morina, N., Powers, M. B., Smits, J. A. J., & Emmelkamp, P. M. G. (2015). A meta-analysis of the efficacy of acceptance and commitment therapy for clinically relevant mental and physical health problems.*Psychotherapy and Psychosomatics*, 84(1), 30–36. https://doi.org/10.1159/000365764

Beck, A. T. (1976).Cognitive therapy and the emotional disorders. International Universities Press.

Butler, A. C., Chapman, J. E., Forman, E. M., & Beck, A. T. (2006). The empirical status of cognitive-behavioral therapy: A review of meta-analyses. *Clinical Psychology Review, 26*(1), 17–31. https://doi.org/10.1016/j.cpr.2005.07.003

Evans, S., Ferrando, S., Findler, M., Stowell, C., Smart, C., & Haglin, D. (2008). Mindfulness-based cognitive therapy for generalized anxiety disorder.*Journal of Anxiety Disorders, 22*(4), 716–721. https://doi.org/10.1016/j.janxdis.2007.07.005

Forman, E. M., Herbert, J. D., Moitra, E., Yeomans, P. D., & Geller, P. A. (2007).A randomized controlled effectiveness trial of acceptance and commitment therapy and cognitive therapy for anxiety and depression.*Behavior Modification, 31*(6), 772–799. https://doi.org/10.1177/0145445507302202

Hayes, S. C., Strosahl, K. D., & Wilson, K. G. (1999). Acceptance and commitment therapy: An experiential approach to behavior change. Guilford Press.

Hofmann, S. G., Sawyer, A. T., & Fang, A. (2010).The empirical status of the "new wave" of cognitive behavioral therapy.*Psychiatric Clinics of North America, 33*(3), 701–710. https://doi.org/10.1016/j.psc.2010.04.006

Holzel, B. K., Carmody, J., Vangel, M., Congleton, C., Yerramsetti, S. M., Gard, T., & Lazar, S. W. (2011). Mindfulness practice leads to increases in regional brain gray matter density. *Psychiatry Research: Neuroimaging, 191*(1), 36–43. https://doi.org/10.1016/j.pscychresns.2010.08.006

Kabat-Zinn, J. (1990). Full catastrophe living: Using the wisdom of your body and mind to face stress, pain, and illness. Delacorte.

Kabat-Zinn, J. (2003). Mindfulness-based interventions in context: Past, present, and future. *Clinical Psychology: Science and Practice, 10*(2), 144–156. https://doi.org/10.1093/clipsy.bpg016

Linehan, M. M. (1993). Cognitive-behavioral treatment of borderline personality disorder.Guilford Press.

Segal, Z. V., Williams, J. M. G., & Teasdale, J. D. (2002). Mindfulness-based cognitive therapy for depression: A new approach to preventing relapse. Guilford Press.

Teasdale, J. D., Segal, Z. V., Williams, J. M. G., Ridgeway, V. A., Soulsby, J. M., & Lau, M. A. (2000). Prevention of relapse/recurrence in major depression by mindfulness-based cognitive therapy.*Journal of Consulting and Clinical Psychology, 68*(4), 615–623. https://doi.org/10.1037/0022-006X.68.4.615

Section III: Technology and Innovation in Education

11

Technological Innovations for Teaching and Learning in Higher Education Institutions

Dr. Kuldeep Kaur Juneja

Assistant Professor, Education Department,
Nirmala College of Education, Ujjain (M.P.) India
Email: kuldpjuneja@gmail.com

Abstract

This paper aims to discuss why and how innovation and Educational Technology need to be integrated, at all levels, to improve learners' meaningful learning. With technology, educators, students, and parents have a variety of learning tools at their fingertips. Technology is essential in all fields, social, political, economic, cultural, spiritual, educational, etc. It has changed the way we think and perceive the situation. Technology has improved education over a span of time. These 21st-century skills are more important to students now than ever before. So, innovation is the core of teaching-learning process and helps to be a good citizen. It enables us to be civically engaged, to develop critical thinking, to be digitally literate, globally aware, and to be effective communicators. Innovation and Educational Technology are regarded as important aspects that would lead to the progression of the system of education. In educational institutions at all levels, instructors are making use of technologies to impart information to students and to develop intellectual skills. In addition, students are encouraged to make use of technologies to prepare their assignments and projects. The members of the educational institutions need to augment their competencies and abilities that would enable them to carry out their tasks effectively and develop the skills of 21st-century learners.

Keywords: *Education, Educational Technology, Innovation, Learning and Teaching.*

Introduction

Educational Technology is making dynamic changes in society and influencing all aspects of life. The influences are being felt more and more at educational institutions. Educational technology provides students and teachers with more opportunities to adapt learning and teaching to students' needs. Society is firmly asking the institutions to actively respond to these technical innovations to bring a dynamic change in society. Most questions about educational technology in education have shifted from *how to use technologies* to understanding *how to teach and learn with technologies.* Today's educational environment is a complex integrity of goals, needs, competing requirements, pressures, and a variety of resources. We are now living in a world of computers, the internet, laptops, mobiles, i -pads, and other technological inventions. We need an educational institution that will give students the training and skills to students to use technology and its inventions as a tool for teaching and self-improvement. 21st century education promotes the expansion of the definition of literacy beyond the reading, writing, and arithmetic that may have guided what we learn in school. Literacy may now include topics such as media, social, political, emotional development, physical fitness/ health, spirituality, and creativity. The need for information and knowledge was provided by books, print media, radio, and later television. In recent times, much advancement has been made in the field of technology. Appropriate computer technology places users in control of their learning. It encourages communicative and collaborative learning and causes an interactive learning process. It is so because the learning process is based on four key roles of the computer: that of *a tool, a tutor, a topic and a thought provider.*

Definition of the Terms Used in the Study

Education: Education is the process of facilitating learning, or the acquisition of knowledge, skills, values, beliefs and habits.

Education Technology: The International Commission on the Development of Education defined Educational Technology as the intellectual and operational efforts to re-arrange, to regroup, or to systematize applications of scientific methods for the organization of equipment and material to optimize the learning process.

Innovation: Innovation is the creation of something that improves the way we live our lives. Innovation is the creation, development, and implementation of a new product, process, or service to improve efficiency, effectiveness, or competitive advantage.

Teaching and learning: Teaching is one of the instruments of education, and its special function is to impart understanding and skill. The main function of teaching is to make learning effective. The learning process would be completed as a result of teaching. So, teaching and learning are very closely related.

Education and Educational Technology

Education is the passport to the future, for tomorrow belongs to those who prepare for it today, and helps us find meaning behind everything, and helps improve life in a massive way. Educational technology is just not the sum of two words. Earlier developments referred to the role of *technology in education,* which signifies the use of audio-visual equipment. Later development recognized the concept of *technology of education,* that is, techniques and methodologies of teaching - learning process. Thus, Educational technology accepts into its fold both technologies in education. Educational technology has three domains of use:

Technology as a tutor (computer gives instructions and guides the user), *Technology as a teaching tool,* and *technology as a learning tool.* When using educational technology, we should be primarily focused on the educational values of the tools and applications we use, how adequate they are in the acquisition of skills and knowledge, also if there is an interaction between users and tools and if we have positive effects in using them. Several authors (Clements and Sarama, 2003; Glaubke, 2007; Dynarski et al., 2007) suggest that we should focus on five areas of software programs that have the potential to strongly influence students' learning experience:

- The educational value of the program.
- It motivates and engages students in learning.
- Ease of use.
- Interactivity between the student and the programs.
- The software program monitors the progress of the student.

Educational technology is a fast-developing discipline in the field of education. Educational technology in its global aspect influences the teacher to develop the skills to become creative, innovative, to develop critical thinking and intellectual thinking, and be a mentor, facilitator, and guide for the new generation.

Innovation and Educational Technology

One of the major aspects that highlights the significance and meaning of innovation and educational technologies is, they contribute to collecting data in terms of responses of students, learning patterns, content access, and a myriad of information on learning effects (Laying & Twyman). NEP 2020 suggests that it is necessary to implement new styles of curriculum, leadership, and teaching strategies that need to be developed in each faculty, which will be supportive of the new school organizations that are emerging. The members of the educational institutions need to do planning, preparation, and revitalization of the process if new patterns of curriculum organization are to be implemented. It is apparent that when changes are brought about in modern and innovative methods, the members of the educational institutions are required to augment their competencies. It is also necessary that individuals need to ensure they make use of modern and innovative methods to promote welfare and productivity (Howard, 1968). The implication of Educational Technology is increasing efficiency in the classroom. The new generation comes to work with these new technologies, which play a vital role in acquiring cognitive knowledge, so educational technologies must be incorporated into future curricula. The application of Educational Technology enhances skills and learning expertise. With the help of new technology comes an explosion of learning and receiving new information, especially on mobile devices for personalized learning.

National Education Policy 2020 envisions an India–centric education system that contributes directly to transforming our nation sustainably into an equitable and vibrant knowledge society by providing high-quality education to all. A holistic development approach is the need of the hour to create awareness and to develop 21st-century skills among learners which will help them in their professional growth and development and also help to meet the challenges in society.

Quality Education and ICT in Education in India

Improving the quality of education and training is a critical issue particular at a time of educational expansion. ICT enhance the Quality Education in several ways by increasing learner motivation and engagements by facilitating the acquisition of basic skills and by enhancing teacher training. ICT also promote the shift to learner centered education. For developing countries ICT have the potential for increasing access to and improving the relevance and quality of education. There is a growing awareness building among the educationist, stake holders, administrators and policy makers on the emerging role of ICT in enhancing the process and outcome of education:

- The National Policy on Education (NPE) 1986, as modified in 1992 stressed on the need of a common entrance examination on all India basis for admission to professional and technical programs in the country.
- The National Curriculum Frame work (NCF) for School Education (2000) rightly remarked, "The new technology has a tremendous potential to revolutionize education and transform school dramatically". The NCF (2005) also highlighted *the significant role of ICT in school education.*
- The Sarva Shiksha Abhiyan (SSA) a mission of the Indian Government to achieve the UEE, also stresses *the importance of ICT in educational sector.*
- The Central Advisory Board of Education (CABE) also in its report on Universal Secondary Education - 2005 featured *the comprehensive use of ICT as one of the most important aspects of schooling.*
- The beaming educational program to satellite was first introduced in our country during the year 1975-76 through the Satellite Instructional Television Experiment (SITE). The vital aim of the INSAT is to bring the rural people into the national mainstream.
- Realizing the importance of ICT (1984-85), the Government of India launched the Computer Literacy and Studies in School (CLASS) Project.
- The Project was adopted as a centrally sponsored scheme during the VIII Plan: 1993-98 (MHRD). The new technology can bring a holistic development in higher education institutions. Hence, a proper knowledge of using ICT and OER in teaching is essential. With the skill and expertise of ICT, the teacher can develop the personality of the students.

Findings

- OECD TALIS study (2013) reports that teachers who report participation in professional development activities involving individual and collaborative research are more likely to report active teaching strategies including the use of ICT.

- Successful schools have shown to have facilitated the use of external research and the navigation of the world of academia in a study by Cooper (2010).
- Strong evidence of links between teacher engagement in and with research and significant changes in practice with a positive impact on student's outcomes were received by Bell et al (2010).
- The "Decoding Learning" report categorized innovations into eight categories based upon the theory of learning Acts (Manches et.al.2010): Learning from Experts, with others, through exploring, inquiry, practicing and assessment. Also learning in and across settings. It can also strengthen future learning by helping learners establish more unique approaches to learning.
- The curriculum and pedagogy of our institutions must develop among the students a deep sense of respect towards the Fundamental Duties and Constitutional values, bonding with one's country, and a conscious awareness of one's roles and responsibilities in a changing world.
- The vision of the policy is to instill among the learners a deep-rooted pride in being Indian, not only in thought, but also in spirit, intellect and deeds, as well as to develop knowledge, skills, values and to be a good citizen of the society.

Recommendations

- Teachers need to be given the opportunities to develop the skills that will enable them to digitally *stick and glue* and create their own resources.
- Teachers need to develop and share ways of using technologies, either through informal collaboration or formal professional development.
- They also need to be given a chance to work with Educational Technology developers from whom they can learn and with whom they can share their expertise of teaching.

Conclusion

We need to recognize a 21st century education is the bedrock of competitiveness in the engine. Improved Technology Enhanced Learning for all in classrooms and home ensures improved learning, better teaching and better research. In order to lead to progression of the system of education in all regions, facilitate the acquisition of education among individuals and enable the members of the educational institutions to carry out their tasks and functions in a well- organized manner, it is necessary to make use of technologies and modern innovative methods. A collaborative learning environment is necessary for effective innovations in teaching and learning because it is clear that no group can develop effective innovations on their own. The need for collaborative relationship is increasingly recognized. Educators need to embrace this new world of resources and consider how they might engage with those outside the classroom within the local community and beyond.

References

Bell, S. (2010) Project-Based Learning for the 21st Century: Skills for the Future. The Clearing House, 83, 39-43.http://dx.doi.org/10.1080/00098650903505415.

Cooper, H. (2010). Research synthesis and meta-analysis: A step-by-step approach (4th ed.). Sage Publications, Inc.

Kapur, R. (2019). Constructivism in Teaching-Learning Process. Delhi: University of Delhi.

Luckin, R, Bligh, B, Manches, A, Ainsworth, S, Crook, C &Noss, R (2012). Decoding Learning: The Proof, Promise and Potential of Digital Education.Nesta.http://www.nesta.org.uk/publications/decoding-learning

Luckin, R. (2015). Mainstreaming Innovation in Educational Technology. Research Gate. *Advances in Scholarship of Teaching and Learning.* 3,(1).ISSN:2382-5855

National Education Policy 2020.

Pisanu, F. (2014). Educational Innovation and Technology: A need for Integration. *Perspectives of Innovations, Economics & Business.*14, (2). ISSN:1804 -0527.

Stosic, L. (2015). The Importance of Educational Technology in Teaching. The *International Journal of Cognitive Research in Science, Engineering and Education* (IJCRSEE).3 (1).

Teaching and Learning. vikaspedia. in> teachers - corner.

12

Role of Virtual Education in COVID-19 Era

Dr. Malabika Borah

Assistant Professor, Department of Chemistry, B. N. College (Autonomous), Dhubri

Email: malabikaborah@gmail.com

Abstract

Most of us grew up with face-to-face learning in a traditional classroom. It is a well-known fact that Covid-19 is presenting to all educational institutions including universities and colleges a challenge to teach students, as infections are known to increase in crowded places. Education of this population, if social distancing requirement is needed, therefore, will be tough. In this context, virtual education plays a crucial role and this is the only way to hold classrooms in the present situation. During this prevailing situation of pandemic, students are forced to engage in online learning, coming out of their usual routine.

Virtual education has both positive and negative aspects. Though it gives the learner more control over when they can learn and allows learners to progress at their own pace; but these aspects are true only for a small portion of students. These are in no way valid for school going students as well as students below 21. Contrary to the positive aspects, virtual education requires less commitment and most importantly, comes with plenty of distractions. Virtual education may be fruitful for higher studies, but cannot fulfill the requirements at the lower basic level for society as well as for the nation.

Keywords: *Pandemic, online teaching and virtual education.*

1. Introduction

The new corona virus Covid-19, first identified in the Chinese city of Wuhan, appears to cause severe acute respiratory syndrome (SARS) and there is evidence that it is originated in bats, leading to more than one crore deaths across the world till date, making WHO to declare it as a pandemic. To regulate the spread of this disease, most of the countries have declared lockdown due to which during this period, global air traffic has dropped by 60%. These emission reductions have led to a temporary dip in carbon-di-oxide emissions, encouraging some to hope that our global society may indeed be able to reduce greenhouse gas emissions substantially over the long term to mitigate impending climate change[1]. So long as the corona virus crisis keeps economic activities reduced, emissions will remain relatively low. However, it would be short-sighted to conclude this is a durable environmental improvement as emissions will most likely rise to previous levels when economic activity picks up as the crisis resolves.

But not all the environmental consequences of the crisis have been positive. Volumes of unrecyclable waste have risen, severe cuts in agricultural and fishery export levels have led to the generation of large quantities of organic waste, maintenance and monitoring of natural ecosystems have been temporarily halted and tourism activity to natural areas has ceased[1].

Covid-19 is creating a challenge to all educational institutions including schools, colleges and universities. Therefore, online teaching plays the most important role for holding classrooms in the current pandemic situation. Though there are both positive and negative perspectives in this virtual education system, in the present scenario, despite of all the negative impacts it may create, it left no way to continue the education of the present youth this way to help them achieving their future goals. It becomes necessary till the present situation persists and the terror of corona completely disappears or till any remedy for the problem is identified.

2. Materials and Methods

The paper involves a detailed study of the present online scenario through a range of survey done with the students, teachers as well as retired professors from schools, colleges and universities in the form of questionnaires covering several dimensions in this area. The questions included the effects on physical and mental health, the art of self-questioning, practicing their secrets, strategies to unlock and unleashing it as well as the need for the inner power in the prevailing situation.

3. Results and Discussion

3.1 Readiness for online education mode

In a country like India, where the percentage of poverty is very high, it is a matter of great concern to deal with the upcoming situation of virtual or online education to every nook and corner of the country. Though the government was planning to implement virtual education system just before the Covid-19 outbreak, it becomes the need of the hour suddenly due to this situation. It is well known that across all over India, only about 52% of students have household internet facility including smart phones and about 28.5% of students have a computer, though urban areas are in a better condition with about 64% having internet and 41% having computer[2]. Thus, to a certain extent only, it may be feasible, at least in the urban areas to impart education through online education system.

Now the government is implementing several schemes through opening of different radio and television channels like specially to incorporate the virtual education in every region of our country so that all the students get benefitted. Offcourse, these schemes are creating a high positive impact on the present need, but for the better benefit of the students, they should also be provided with the required equipment in need as well as internet facilities if possible.

3.2 Virtual over conventional

Most of us grew up with face-to-face learning in a traditional classroom. But during this prevailing situation of Covid-19 pandemic, students are forced to engage in online learning, coming out of their usual routine. Otherwise, earlier, if they want to learn something that is not as available in college, then only they need to explore alternative means like an online course where they are teaching themselves using the provided materials.

Face-to-face education means a live, two-way interaction whereas online education mean anything that doesn't include a live instructor. So, online education is where a student sits down and learns through a self-paced system, completely on their own. There might be content delivered through video, but it is a one-way interaction. Though it gives the learner more control over when they can learn, allows learners to progress at their own pace and does not subject learners to distractions from others; but these aspects are true only for a small portion of students excluding the school students. In addition, for the subjects where field works as well as lab works are required, virtual education cannot really fulfill the needs.

In a face-to-face education system, at least one knows whether the learners are expecting to learn or not. So we are able to get an idea about **their advancement. But in online education system, it becomes difficult to note down exactly the status of the learners.** Contrary to the positive aspects, virtual education requires less commitment, might lead learners to falsely think they are ready to progress and comes with plenty of distractions through various sites available on the internet.

To rectify the possible negative aspects, one has to develop certain restrictive means in internet through which distractions can be completely removed. Secondly, prior to the online learning, the students would require an offline mentor that will continuously keep an eye to the overall progress of the students. The mentor may be a teacher or a family member specially in case of school-going students. Thus, not only for the present situation, virtual education system may become a fruitful one if maintained in a proper way erasing out all the possible negative aspects.

3.3 E-resources

E-resources can be defined as a group of informations disseminated in electronic or digital format, which is produced, published and distributed electronically. It comes from the use of the internet and related technologies for its development, distribution and enhancement. To access electronic resources, networked computers are necessary ingredients that any university or college should strive to have. It is established that about 75% of the respondents depend on the university or college to access networked computers, only about 18% believe these resources provided easier access to information. This might be attributed to the lack of available personal computers because of which though e-resources can be read in both online and offline mode, the full utilization of it becomes limited.

But even though, open access initiative has made it easier to reach in the hands of an individual information seeker. These e-resources cover entire universe of knowledge which includes arts, humanities, commerce, law, social sciences, physical sciences, chemical sciences, life sciences, computer sciences, engineering, mathematical sciences, medical sciences etc. So there are no areas left untouched. The fruitful utilization of e-resources will possible only by motivating the students for its maximum utilization.

Further, 100% of the respondents propose that more networked computers should be purchased by the university or colleges to help students to access e-resources. It is also significant that about 33% of the students do not consider that access to quality information via e-resources can lead to improved academic performance. Therefore, to popularize the use of e-resources, some awareness measures may be developed so that the students can able to understand the wide utility and benefits of e-resources available through open access which will really help our government to achieve the required goals of taking such initiatives.

3.4 Internet access

Internet can be described as a tremendous source of information now-a-days. Access to the Internet is fundamental to achieving this vision for the future. It can be regarded as a world of information and access to the Internet is essential for the purpose. However, lack of access is first and foremost problem arise in this context. Lack of connectivity is preventing widespread use of internet in education in many countries including India.

Our survey concludes if somehow the problem of connectivity is resolved, yet the internet can be used both in a positive and negative manner. This may act as a useful tool for a student by giving them opportunity to acquire knowledge in whatever field they want. As a result the students are capable to achieve their goal as per their desire. But at the same time, they have a wide range of distractions also. There are several sites available which are of no use at any angle. The students may be distracted and they may lose their concentration in achieving their goal. In that case, internet may be a dangerous threat to the upcoming youth to shape their future in a good way.

3.5 Effect on health

In the present scenario of Covid-19 pandemic, every institution is trying to reach out to the maximum number of students through online mode conducting online classes as well as keeping them busy with several other programmes so that they can adopt this unusual situation. While doing so, the students are compelled to spend several hours a day in mobile or computer. As no one has the idea about the maximum hours that a student should spend in these activities, the institutions are conducting classes without any time limit.

As a result of his, most of the students are suffering from health problems such as headache, gastric as well as spondylitis. Continuation of such activities for a longer time may lead to major health problems. Therefore, this should find an important concern in conducting virtual education system for a long duration specially in the present situation. There should be some time limitation of online classes for smooth running of the system.

In addition, due to poor network connectivity in most of the rural area in our country as well as due to some natural calamity, the smooth continuation of the online activities is also got hampered some time. This also creates anxiety and tension as well as depression among the students affecting their mental health also.

3.6 Lack of physical activities

We know that physical activities play a vital role in maintaining both our physical and mental health. Because of the lockdown going on, the students are forced to remain inside their homes and as a result, they are not able to do their routine physical tasks. Therefore at this phase of corona pandemic, they should be encouraged to continue any type of physical activities which not only will create a positive health effect, but also will boost up immunity to fight against this situation. This will also increase their interest for the ongoing virtual education system simultaneously.

3.7 Innovation through virtual mode

As the online teaching and learning is the only way left in the prevailing scenario, the teachers need more to innovate new ideas and techniques to pursue the students' interests more making the process much more exciting. For example, they may try to implement new softwares and applications such as Gimkit, Socrative, nearpod etc. which may build interest of the students in a particular topic through gamification of education.

3.8 Introduction to extra-curricular activities

In addition to the regular curriculum, some extra-curricular activities may be introduced to the students which may be related to their individual hobbies such as singing, playing with different instruments, creative writings in the form of poems, stories etc. This type of practice will not only help the students to discover their individual hidden talents but also will act as a vitamin to their physical as well as their mental health.

4. Conclusion

Though in the present situation of Covid-19 pandemic, virtual education gives a new direction to our existing conventional education system, it can be implemented successfully in future days also. Though it cannot just replace the conventional system, but it can prove to be a highly beneficial support to the existing education system. Exposure to the benefits of virtual education is necessary in today's world but its potential can only be utilized well through a proper systematic way with limitation in timeline.

Virtual education may be fruitful for higher studies, giving the students a wide variety of choices that may not be possible to achieve conventionally. At a time, virtual education system gives the students a great opportunity to fulfill their expected destinations. However, it cannot fulfill the requirements at the lower basic level in any way. But it can be stated that conventional with additional virtual education system will really help the students to achieve their desired goals if they are highly determined.

References

Hamwey, R. (2020).Environmental impacts of corona virus crisis, challenges ahead. *UNCTAD*.https://unctad.org/news/environmental-impacts-coronavirus-crisis-challenges-ahead

Indian National Commission for cooperation with UNESCO response to COVID 19, 2020.https://www.education.gov.in/sites/upload_files/mhrd/files/inccu_0.pdf

Internet Access and Education: Key considerations for policy makers, *Public Policy*, 2017. https://www.internetsociety.org/resources/doc/2017/internet-access-and-education/

Internet Society report, Promoting Local Content Hosting to Develop the Internet Ecosystem,http://www.internetsociety.org/doc/promoting-local-content-hosting-develop-internet-ecosystem

Waykar, A., Waykar, Y. (2016).A study of mobile internet users in India. *PARIPEX-Indian Journal of Research*, 5(4).https://www.worldwidejournals.com/paripex/article/a-study-of-mobile-internet-users-in-india/Mjk2MTY=/?is=1&b1=377&k=95

13

From Traditional to Flipped Classroom: A Systematic Review of Pedagogical Shifts and Contemporary Applications in India

LikhaYadi

Ph.D. Scholar, Department of Education,
Rajiv Gandhi University, Arunachal Pradesh
Email: yadilikha998@gmail.com

Abstract

The flipped classroom is a shift of pedagogical approach from traditional to modern. The shift in pedagogy, changing from teacher-centered to student-centered approaches and from passive learning to cooperative learning, represents a more profound change in how knowledge is developed, disseminated, and applied. Emergence factors of online learning, such as active learning, flexible learning environments, personalized learning pathways, active learning strategies, and peer collaboration, are the result of the increased effectiveness of flipped classrooms. However, shifting to a flipped classroom also has challenges, including the digital divide among different sections of the population, especially those who reside in rural regions; the lack of fully digitally literate students and teachers; the existing traditional classroom infrastructure; etc.

Keywords: *Active Learning, Flipped Classroom, Pedagogical shifts, Student Engagement, Technology Integration*

1. Introduction

Integration of information technology in pedagogy has been has been used in education since the 20th century, but in the 21st century, it has become overly involved. Examples of this include learning management systems (LMS), gamification tools, artificial intelligence (AI) and adaptive learning, video-based learning, assessment tools, mobile learning apps, etc. Because new issues require innovative answers, many educators and policymakers advocated blended learning as an alternative for educational institutions, particularly during and after the COVID-19 pandemic. This approach enables students to learn outside of the conventional classroom, particularly in situations where face-to-face instruction is not feasible. In regular teaching learning model, lecture, demonstration, tutorial, practical, clinical, and field posts are frequent teaching-learning techniques that are augmented with seminars, student symposia, debate, role play, and panel discussion but as a perception that a new graduate must be able to develop essential skills in order to deliver socially responsive care arises increasingly, the flipped classroom emerges as one of the prominent models (**Ramesh & Chetan, 2021**).

Historically, India's pedagogy has evolving from relying solely on the teacher to impart knowledge to students through the use of shravana (oral transmission), manana (reflection), and nididhyasan (meditation) from guru to shishya in ancient times; being dialogic and experiential in medieval times, with the teacher at the center and students still learning passively; lecture-based teaching and the exam approach during the colonial era; and transitioning to a student-centered approach in the modern era by emphasizing students' competencies and allowing for greater flexibility in learning. Following the 2019 pandemic, in India, all of these online learning concepts have gained a lot of popularity. One of which is Flipped classroom method of teaching. Developed nations are more likely to adopt the flipped classroom approach.

The flipped classroom is a shift of pedagogical approach from traditional to modern. The 'flipped classroom' has been defined as "a set of pedagogical approaches that seek to reduce student cognitive load and increase student motivation and engagement by moving most information-transmission teaching out of class, using class time for learning activities that are both active and social, and requiring students to complete pre and/or post-class activities to fully benefit from in-class work" **Abeysekera & Dawson, 2014**. It has come out as one of these approaches, bringing changes in traditional educational frameworks by reversing the typical teaching at classroom and homework components of a course. The implementation of a flipped classroom approach involves requiring students to engage with interactive content focussing on key concepts prior to attending class, so that during class time they can participate in collaborative activities that clarify concepts and contextualise knowledge through application, analysis and problem solving (**Karanicolas & Snelling, 2010**). The shift to flipped classroom is shifting teacher centred to student centred. In this teaching learning approach, learners receive lesson content prior the class, often through online videos or reading assignments, and then using class time for interactive discussion, application-oriented learning activities. According to **Cambridge Dictionary**, it is a teaching method in which students first learn about a new subject at home, especially online, and then have discussions on it in class. This strategy emphasizes students, encouraging their active participation, critical analysis, and team learning. In addition to altering students' conventional learning styles, it has also altered teachers'. Online learning factors such as active learning, flexible learning environments, personalized learning pathways, active learning strategies, and peer collaboration are the result of the increased effectiveness of flipped classrooms.

In the flipped classroom approach, the teacher, by using an online platform, distributes the prepared learning contents, and students study them prior to class time and use the class period for discussing the contents they self-studied. Some key important tools used in a flipped classroom are i. video lectures, which are lectures that have been recorded and are accessible to students at their own leisure with the option to pause, fast-forward, and revisit, and are among the key resources utilized in a flipped classroom. ii. Interactive Simulations: Virtual environments that provide hands-on, interactive learning experiences. iii. Reading Materials: Digital textbooks, articles, and other online reading materials **(Shambhavi, 2024)**. Traditionally, teachers prepare the lesson for the upcoming classes primarily offline by writing it down on paper, creating Xerox copies, and using the book directly, and after the emergence of smart classrooms, PPT was also used for lesson dissemination. Students are passive recipients in the traditional model. They totally depend on teachers for the content knowledge. In this convention model the teachers use the whole class period for lecture and writing, and the homework is given for post-class time.

Shifting pedagogy is not just merely to address technological progress; it aims to re-evaluate the theories and practices of teaching, learning, and evaluation. It equips students not just to succeed in an information-abundant world, but it focuses more on developing students cognitive and critical thinking to solve practical world issues. According to Buckman et al. (2010), there are four key tactics for active learning: (1) design individual activities both inside and outside of the classroom; (2) involve students in group activities; (3) encourage unstructured group work; and (4) give cooperative students project-based work. The flipped classroom approach exactly focuses on those key tactics. Under the direction of the teacher, this new model of teaching strategy enables students to participate in active learning techniques, including open discussion, group projects, and peer evaluation. They learn new content at home, and that learned material becomes the base for students to have increasingly complex and interactive exercises in class time. Students study more independently in a flipped learning environment.

The shift in pedagogy, changing from teacher-centered to student-centered approaches and from passive learning to cooperative learning, represents a more profound change in how knowledge is developed, disseminated, and applied. The teacher-centered approach has dominated most academic environments for many decades. Since the teacher is the only source of knowledge in this approach, students are supposed to passively receive the information that is presented to them. Students are expected to memorize and reproduce the material they have studied, as well as cover the predetermined curriculum within a given time frame. This places the teacher at the center of the learning process and gives them authority and decision-making power, which limits students' opportunities for creativity, critical thinking, and self-expression.

2. Objectives and Methodology

The relevant data used in this research paper, "From Traditional to Flipped Classroom: A Systematic Review of Pedagogical Shifts and Contemporary Applications in India," came from secondary sources, such as reports, studies, popular websites, and previously completed research publications. This systematic review will therefore focus more on accomplishing the following goals.

1. To examine how the shift from traditional to flipped classroom model has improved student performance.
2. To assess the benefits and challenges of flipped classrooms in the Indian context.

3. Findings and Discussions

After reviewing some of the existing studies it is found that the flipped classroom, fosters active participation, critical thinking, problem-solving skills, self-evaluation and team learning in teaching and learning process. Many of the studies' findings indicate that this approach gives more positive learning outcomes. By offering students more flexible learning environment, this new model of learning is set to play a central role in the evolving landscape of education. It also shows the growing adoption of flipped classroom approach in the Indian education scenario, efforts of pedagogical application, and the related educational technology to access (**Azhar&Rashid, 2024**). By saying that the success of flipped classrooms depends heavily on the caliber and layout of the digital learning resources (**Al-Samarraie et al., 2019**). To produce interesting, dynamic, and pedagogically sound digital resources that support the learning objectives, instructors must devote a significant amount of time and energy (**Rotellar& Cain, 2016**).

3.1. Benefits of Flipped Classroom Models

Its student-focused approach allows students to develop more independent problem-solving skills, critical thinking, and creativity. Unlike the traditional model, where students are solely dependent on the teacher for the lesson, which restricts students from exploring apart from predefined content. It allows self-paced learning for students and benefits students who need extra time to grasp the lesson. Students can access the study material and can learn at anytime, anywhere, at any pace. As students study prior to the class, this frees up class time to concentrate on higher-level skills like application, analysis, and evaluation.

A class time can be used for more individualized learning by discussing the doubts one-on-one with the teacher, which was not feasible in a normal classroom due to time constraints.

Students utilize in-class time for debates, problem-solving, and a more thorough examination of the material after accessing instructional content, such as online resources or video lectures, outside of class (Peisachovich et al., 2016).Its integration of multimedia into the teaching-learning process makes learning more interesting and helps students be more active in the learning process. It keeps students more active in the learning process, as they have to do continuous self-study and evaluation before coming to the main classroom.

This cooperative learning environment allows students to develop socially, emotionally, and empathetically and to learn teamwork.

3.2. Challenges and Limitations in the Indian Context

Despite various initiatives of the government of India on internet inclusivity, many youths, especially those who reside in rural regions and come from low-economy backgrounds, still lack proper internet connection. For this section of students, the flipped classroom is not a fit. The success of the flipped classroom approach depends on the efficient integration of digital tools and technologies (**ShambhaviKumari, 2024**).

Implementation of a flipped classroom demands a significant investment of time for pre-class preparation from both teacher and students. Teachers may become discouraged by this increased burden, especially those who are new to digital tools. They have to prepare pre-study materials, and students might also find it challenging while trying to cover the content before class. Overuse of technology can make students highly dependent on it and feel it is not necessary to attend class for face-to-face interaction.

Not every student has the same ability; likewise, some may find it difficult to switch to the flipped classroom method, especially if they are used to a more conventional learning approach where they first learn content from the teacher and then do the homework. This model will be successful only if both teachers and students are fully equipped with digital literacy and technical abilities, often requiring further training to manage classrooms effectively. As study materials are provided online, it might lead to overuse of screen time. The teacher will need to put in more time and effort for preparing study materials than usual. They have to prepare lesson plans and PPTs, record videos, and create quizzes for tracking the students' level of study and understanding of content, then collect the reviews and accordingly tailor the discussion point for each level of students.

3.3. Contemporary Applications in Indian Education

21st-century students' instructional models demand that information and communication technology (ICT) be integrated. The flipped classroom integrates collaborative technologies to support student engagement, knowledge co-creation, and the development of essential 21st-century skills, such as communication, collaboration, and critical thinking, by utilizing tools like document editors, virtual whiteboards, and video conferencing platforms that enable real-time collaboration, interactive activities, and peer review even when students are not physically present. (**Kumari, 2024**). In order to fit in the modern trend of education in today's world that is changing quickly, the Indian educational system is embracing the changes by adopting these emerging innovative methods that enhance the quality of education and equip students for upcoming problems. This shift from traditional teaching methods to a more interactive, student-centered approach is a significant shift in educational practice. By implementing this revolutionary method that uses technology to facilitate active, group, and personalized learning, the curriculum is being revamped to foster creativity, critical thinking, and practical skills by taking into account each child's needs and interests. This more individualized learning experience, higher course memory, and better student performance are all possible outcomes of this change in instructional design. With the growing prevalence of smartphones among students in India in today's digital era, the flipped classroom approach appears to be a viable method to adopt. Because smartphones can serve as important accessible tools for delivering lessons and have access to readily available educational videos on the internet. In response to these, NEP 2020 emphasizes integrating digital technology into every level of education. It developed platforms like NPTEL and SWAYAM DIKSHA to deliver high-quality e-learning by focusing on the use of digital in learning.

According to the Economic Times, the Indian School of Business (ISB) was one of the first management schools in the nation to implement the "flipped classroom" to instruct students in a course on making entrepreneurial decisions in 2013. Following that, it began to receive attention from all academic fields as a result of its ability to create interactive classrooms, which is currently a necessity for students of this era **(Malik & Rani, 2023)**. However, due to the unique socio-cultural and educational landscape of India, it presents both opportunities and challenges for the effective integration of flipped learning into mainstream education. Despite its potential, the implementation and research on the flipped learning approach in India remain limited and fragmented **(Azhar& Rashid, 2024)**.

4. Conclusion

Based on the discussions, it is concluded that the flipped classroom method has the potential of fostering deeper learning due to its student-centered and flexible approach. It fosters more critical thinking skills in students by involving them in active learning. By using both online and face-to-face modes of teaching in the classroom, it makes learning more accessible and convenient as compared with traditional methods. However, shifting to a flipped classroom also has challenges, including the digital divide among different sections of the population, especially those who reside in rural regions; the lack of fully digitally literate students and teachers; the existing traditional classroom infrastructure; etc. Therefore, in order to successfully implement the flipped classroom approach at all levels of educational institutions, the existing challenges need to be taken care of. Additionally, the government has to strictly inspect the existing initiatives it has developed in these areas.

References

Abeysekera, L., & Dawson, P. (2015). Motivation and cognitive load in the flipped classroom: Definition, rationale, and a call for research. *Higher Education Research & Development*, 34(1), 1–14. https://doi.org/10.1080/07294360.2014.934336

AlsancakSirakaya, D., & Ozdemir, S. (2018). The effect of a flipped classroom model on academic achievement, self-directed learning readiness, motivation, and retention.*International Journal of Educational Technology in Higher Education*, 15(1), 1–16. https://eric.ed.gov/?id=EJ1165484

Azhar, A., & Rashid, R. A. (2024). Flipped learning approach in India: A systematic literature review. *International Journal for Multidisciplinary Research*, 6(4).https://doi.org/10.36948/ijfmr.2024.v06i04.26708

Clark, K. R., & Falls, W. (2013). Examining the effects of the flipped model of instruction on student engagement and performance in the secondary mathematics classroom: An action research study. *Journal of Educators Online*, 12, 91–115.

Divjak, B., Rienties, B., Iniesto, F., Vondra, P., & Žižak, M. (2022). Flipped classrooms in higher education during the COVID-19 pandemic: Findings and future research recommendations. *International Journal of Educational Technology in Higher Education*, 19(1), 1–24.

Fraga, L. M., & Harmon, J. (2015). The flipped classroom model of learning in higher education: An investigation of preservice teachers' perspectives and achievement. *Journal of Digital Learning in Teacher Education*, 31(1), 18–27. https://doi.org/10.1080/21532974.2014.967420

Gunbatar, M. S. (2021). Flipped classroom in higher education: Evaluation of the process in the framework of community of inquiry. *Journal of Educational Technology Systems*, 50(2), 215–254. https://doi.org/10.1177/00472395211031660

Kumari, S. (2024). The role of technology in flipped classrooms: Enhancing learning through digital tools. *ShikshaSahitya International Peer Reviewed Research Journal*, 10(1), 1–12.https://www.researchgate.net/publication/388313944

Maheshwari, P. and Seth, N. (2019), Effectiveness of flipped classrooms: A case of management education in central India. *International Journal of Educational Management*, Vol. 33 No. 5, pp. 860-885. https://doi.org/10.1108/IJEM-10-2017-0282

Malik, M., & Rani, R. (2023). Flipped classroom in India before and after COVID-19: A systematic review. *International Journal for Research Trends and Innovation*, 8(6), 523–538. https://ijrti.org/papers/IJRTI2306081.pdf

Ramesh, L., & Chethan. (2021). The impacts of the flipped classroom on students' academic achievement. *International Journal of Creative Research Thoughts*, 9(10), 523–530. https://ijcrt.org/papers/IJCRT2110060.pdf

Strelan, P., Osborn, A., & Palmer, E. (2020). The flipped classroom: A meta-analysis of effects on student performance across disciplines and education levels. *Educational Research Review*, 30, 100314.https://doi.org/10.1016/j.edurev.2020.100314

Van Vliet, E. A., Winnips, J. C., & Brouwer, N. (2015). Flipped-class pedagogy enhances student metacognition and collaborative-learning strategies in higher education but effect does not persist. *CBE Life Sciences Education*, 14(3), ar26. https://doi.org/10.1187/cbe.14 09-0141

14

The Transformative Impact of Artificial Intelligence on Personalized Learning in Higher Education

Saurav Bhaumik[1] **& Kigo Raksap**[2]

[1]Student, (MA Education), *Rajiv Gandhi University, Arunachal Pradesh*
[2]*Student, (MA Education), Rajiv Gandhi University, Arunachal Pradesh*
Email: bhaumiksaurav349@gmail.com

Abstract

Personalized learning means using learning experiences that match each student's unique needs, preferences and abilities. The study explorers the ways in which Artificial Intelligence (AI) is bringing transformation to personalized learning in higher education. With AI, it is possible to use adaptive classrooms, profile learners using data, design intelligent tutoring tools and test students automatically. The presence of AI in education has been related to better student participation, better learning achievement, wider access and efficient use of time. At the same time, bringing AI into use raises major concerns, for example, privacy with data, possible practical biases from algorithms, faded transparency and increasing dependence on automated systems rather than interacting with others. The study looks at new trends, including advanced AI models, linking several types of data and personalized use of analytics, while reminding readers of the role ethical AI plays. The conclusion urges cooperation among teachers, tech experts and officials to see that AI is responsibly and equally introduced at colleges and universities.

Keywords: *Personalized learning, artificial intelligence, and higher education.*

Introduction

The people and organizations in higher education are experiencing unprecedented transformation as emerging digital tools are being used more widely. AI is standing out from the others by changing teaching methods and bringing in innovative ways for students and teachers. AI's support for personalized learning is greatly changing higher education by offering solutions created to suit every student's abilities, interests and needs. With more institutions using AI in education, it is now easier to improve learning, education experiences and increase equality. For many years, educators have tried to achieve personalized learning, making learning activities suitable for each person. Even so, traditional schooling which depends on similar learning content and standard ways of testing has been unable to truly personalize learning for all students.

AI is making it more likely that this vision will become a reality. By using machine learning, natural language processing, data analytics and intelligent systems, AI allows teachers to handle personal tutoring, guess at student needs and respond quickly with personalized responses. The section discusses in detail how AI and personalized learning are connected in higher education. This field investigates what personalized learning and AI truly mean, describes actual applications of these technologies in schools, notes the advantages for students and teachers and pays close attention to the ethical, logistical and teaching concerns that come up during implementation. Part of the discussion deals with what's to come, including multimodal systems and ethics, giving insights on how institutions can adjust for AI-backed learning ahead.

Concept of Personalised learning and Artificial Intelligence

Personalized learning is about adapting education to suit each person's specific requirements, likes, talents and interests. Because of educational technology and information about each student, personalized learning helps students study according to their individual needs. AI and similar technologies help provide personalized learning by tracking students' progress, supplying tailored feedback, adjusting content and providing interventions. It lets teachers help students catch up on approved points, get interested in learning and do better at school. The use of adaptive learning platforms and intelligent tutoring systems (ITS) has demonstrated that these technologies greatly help students remain engaged and remember what they learn.

Merino-Campos (2025) points out that there's more to personalized learning than just picking your own subjects in college. AI recommendation systems, learning analytics and predictive models are designed to assist with studying as well as with gaining skills to study alone. With AI, those who struggle in education can now access learning materials and lessons the same as everyone else.

Artificial intelligence (AI) means that machines are able to replicate how humans use their intelligence. The subject studies ways to make machines capable of solving issues, learning, using reasoning and choosing like humans. Among its parts, machine learning and natural language processing belong to AI, as these enable computers to learn and speak to humans using language. Artificial intelligence is influencing the way people do their jobs and store data in healthcare, finance, transport and entertainment. Artificial Intelligence is concerned with building machines that are able to work like humans. It involves learning from data, dealing with natural language, spotting patterns, making judgments and tackling problems alone. Possibilities for AI include standard decision trees, neural networks and giant language models. Artificial intelligence is applied in education to create special tutoring systems, complete administrative duties more easily, analyze learning information, offer adaptable learning resources and provide feedback that is suited to each individual. In colleges, these technologies help learning spaces react to the changing needs of each student.

Objectives of the Study

1. To study the transformative power of AI in advancing personalized learning in higher education.

2. To study the benefits of AI-driven personalized learning in higher education.
3. To study the challenges and ethical considerations of artificial intelligence on personalized learning in higher education.
4. To study the emerging trends and future directions of artificial intelligence on personalized learning in higher education.

Methodology of the Study

The study is totally based on secondary sources of data that is available from other published data. Secondary resources, including academic papers, journals, government files, books, websites and newspapers, are used to collect this data. As the study is descriptive in nature, it focuses on organizing knowledge and providing an overview of the topic by summarizing what has been written or done without trying to collect other data or experiment.

Analysis and Discussion

Analysis and discussion have been provided systematically based on the objectives.

Objective 1: To Study the Transformative Power of AI in Advancing Personalized Learning in Higher Education.

Personalization, flexibility and scale all rely on AI in the new approach to education. Listed below are the essential AI-supported technologies shaping personalized learning in colleges and universities.

1. Adaptive learning environment

AI helps learning environments change the way they teach based on how well students are doing and what type of behavior they display. The systems always keep an eye on each student's growth, changing the tasks' difficulty, suggesting useful resources and immediately providing feedback. Because of this approach, students are less likely to tune out from material that is too easy or become bothered by material that is too tough. Gligorea (2023) indicates that the use of adaptive learning in online learning reduced dropouts by 18%. It reveals that AI helps students retain knowledge and pass their courses because it delivers relevant interventions for every student.

2. Intelligent Tutoring Systems (ITS)

ITS are technology tools that help students by providing them with personalized tutoring. They observe the student's actions as they happen, discover areas the student does not understand and immediately provide support. There are systems that act in a Socratic way by asking thoughtful questions to encourage thinking things through. Larger classes benefit greatly from these systems, since not all learners can get as much help from teachers as they wish. ITS helps students become better learners by giving interactive solutions, useful feedback and encouraging motivation(Bit et al. , 2024).

3. Analysing Learners and Constructing Profiles

AI tools can gather and review large numbers of data concerning students' learning habits, tastes and past academic results. Using learning analytics, schools can create detailed profiles of learners which guide improvements to courses, services for students and teaching techniques. AI tools could list learning modalities (e.g., visual, auditory), the length of time students spend on their work, involvement in tasks and their achievement levels. Jiali et al. (2024) Stated that this information is essential for giving students personalized education and helping them before they drop out or fail to keep up.

4. Intelligent tutoring System

AI is able to pick and provide learning materials according to what a student is currently working on. It can involve directing the student to practice videos, educational articles or simulations that suit their challenges or ambitions. Intelligent tutor explains that having recommendation systems in LMSs automatically recommends personal learning resources just as Netflix recommends videos and YouTube makes playlists. It gives students a chance to grow and learn on their own by looking at more than the main curriculum.

5. Personalized Recommendation

With AI algorithms, educators can match education resources such as readings, videos, forums or MOOCs, to students based on their history, interests and goals. As a result, students can access extra materials that increase their learning and knowledge. These suggestions support learning and also foster students' desire to learn and direct their own studies in school.

6. Automated assessment and feedback

AI can assess both facts and emotions with greater ability every day. Using AI, teachers can have automated multiple-choice quizzes graded, detect possible plagiarism and use natural language processing for essay feedback.Using automated feedback systems, students can see what they did wrong and improve fast which reduces the teachers' workload. The result allows teachers to concentrate on helping students through mentoring and explanation of difficult concepts.

Objective 2: To Study the Benefits of AI-Driven Personalized Learning in Higher Education.

AI in learning environments leads to many positive results for students, educators and institutions.

1. Enhanced Student Engagement and Motivation

Personalized learning helps people learn better and stay interested by fitting the lessons to their needs and how they like to study. Being given material that suits what the students want and are good at keeps them motivated and interested. Because of AI,

Adaptive Content adjusts both its content and how quickly it offers it which makes students experience less frustration and boredom. Studies have found that this method boosts both the rate at which learners finish their studies and their pleasure with their learning.

2. Improve learning outcomes

Customizing learning to each student with AI prepares them to understand and learn better. Support provided using adaptive interventions reaches students when and where needed, helping them better understand material and study it correctly. Because of the feedback found in AI-powered systems, students are more likely to ponder their learning choices, check how they are improving and control their own path in learning.

3. Increased Accessibility and Equity

Technologies based on AI can be customized for all types of learners and those with disabilities. Thanks to text-to-speech, speech-to-text, translation and adjustable interfaces, educational tools can be used by students who have vision, hearing, thinking or language difficulties. Because learning is more accessible, students from various backgrounds can work with curriculum that suits them.

4. Optimized Instructor Workload

With AI handling grading and distributing content, teachers find more time to help students, talk with them and develop their lessons. As a result, educators can interact more closely with their students and give better support.

5. Data-Driven Decision-Making

AI-based analysis tools help educators and administrators better understand learning habits, the success of different courses and how students are performing. This information can guide how teachers teach, what skills are assessed and how the institution is run.

Objective 3: To Study the Challenges and Ethical Considerations of Artificial Intelligence on Personalized Learning in Higher Education.

Although AI can improve personalized learning, combining them is not always easy. They have to be managed by careful planning, respecting ethics and engaging stakeholders.

1. Data Privacy and security

Information about each student is collected and used often in personalized learning. There are serious worries about data privacy, permission and ensuring cyber security in this area. Both data security and clear details on how information is processed and kept should be key in any institution. Make sure to meet the requirements of the GDPR and FERPA, as these rules help protect students and prevent people from losing trust.

2. Algorithmic Bias and Fairness

AI may reinforce or raise existing biases when trained with data that reflects bias. Some systems use algorithms to suggest things that may support stereotypes or form barriers for minorities when choosing what to learn. Resolving these issues needs collections of data from a variety of backgrounds, ongoing testing of algorithms and fairness considerations in education design to treat all learners equally.

3. The "Black Box" Problem

Problems of Household Finance can be comprehended due to transparency, but sometimes this idea is seen as a "Black Box." Darkens, constant views are often seen in deep learning AI, meaning a lack of understanding about why decisions are taken. Because information is hidden, students and teachers may find it difficult to trust or hold each other responsible. AI systems must be created in a way that helps users understand, question and check their results. Using Explainable AI (XAI) methods is a possible answer being investigated.

4. Over-Reliance on Technology

Artificial intelligence can change education, but it should not be used to replace personal contact, advice or emotional assistance. Holistic learning for students depends greatly on discussion, collaborating with peers and learning to build meaningful relationships. Bit et al. (2024), stated that we should use AI as a help, not a complete replacement for teaching by people.

5. Implementation Complexity and Cost

The deployment of AI systems requires substantial investments in infrastructure, training, and technical support. Many institutions, particularly in low-resource settings, may struggle with the costs and complexity of integration. Furthermore, faculty must be trained not only in using these systems but also in interpreting AI-generated insights to inform pedagogical decisions.

Objective 4: To Study the Emerging Trends and Future Directions of AI on Personalised Learning in Higher Education.

Several new trends and ideas are changing the face of personalized learning at universities because AI is always advancing,

1. Advanced AI Systems and Language Models

With the appearance of big language models such as GPT-4, personalized learning takes on a whole new character. They are capable of creating language-based guidance, simulating educational chat and supporting learners studying a variety of subjects. Yigci et al. (2024), LLMs are able to be fine-tuned so they provide feedback and suggestions that match a student's language and how well they understand.

2. Multimodal Artificial Intelligence and Emotional Intelligence

Future systems may use information from facial expressions, voice tone, eye movement and physiology to know more about how students are feeling and learning. Yoo et al. (2023), these systems might immediately recognize whether a student is stressed, confused or bored and modify teaching instruction. A system with emotional intelligence would likely become more thoughtful, respond better and achieve its tasks successfully.

3. Intelligent Curriculum Design

Artificial intelligence supports the development of specially designed curricula for specific groups, learning targets and individuals. This means creating the order of content, assigning activities that fit the expected competencies and choosing the best assessment tasks.

4. Personalized Learning Dashboards

By using AI, student-facing dashboards show learners clear and real-time updates about their achievements, areas where they excel and places where they could improve. They allow users to set goals, manage their actions and consider their progress.

5. Ethical AI Frameworks

Because AI is being included in education more often, it will become necessary to create ethical frameworks. Such policies must ensure fairness, accountability, transparency and oversight by human beings. Having experts in technology, ethics, education and policy cooperate is very important

Conclusion

Artificial Intelligence can drive important changes in personalized education for students in higher education. The results from this study show that many researchers are still exploring how AI can enhance learning for students with adaptive tools, engaging activities and unbiased assessment. Even so, introducing AI into personalized learning is not always easy. The topics of data confidentiality, algorithmic unfairness, oversight by humans and problems with implementation deserve close attention and need to be handled. With AI advancing, it is important for educators, policy leaders and developers to team up so the use of AI in colleges and universities remains ethical, fair and helps all students improve their learning. The development of AI is strongly guiding the future of higher education and making the most of its potential will help create new, customised ways of learning.

References

AI-Zahrani, A. M., & Alasmari, T. M. (2024).Exploring the impact of artificial intelligence on higher education: The dynamic of ethical, social and educational implications. *Humanities & Social Science Communication.*

Ayeni, O. O., Hamad, N. M. al, Chisom, O. N., Osawaru, B., Adewusi, O. E., Ayeni, O. O., Hamad, N. M. al, Chisom, O. N., Osawaru, B., & Adewusi, O. E. (2024). AI in education: A review of personalized learning and educational technology. *GSC Advanced Research and Reviews*, 18(2), 261–271. https://doi.org/10.30574/GSCARR.2024.18.2.006.

Bit, D., Biswas, S. & Nag, M. (2024).The impact of artificial intelligence in educational system. *International Journal of Scientific Research and Technology*. 11(4), 419-427.

Chu HC, Hwang GH, Tu YF, Yang KH (2022). Roles and research trends of artificial intelligence in higher education: A systematic review of the top 50most-cited articles. *Australasian Journal of Educational Technology,*38(3):22–42.

Garito, M. A. (1991). Artificial intelligence in education: evolution of the teaching—learning relationship. *British Journal of Educational Technology*, 22(1), 41–47. https://doi.org/10.1111/J.1467-8535.1991.TB00050.X.

Gligorea, I., Cioca, M., Oancea, R., Gorski, A., Gorski, H., & Tudorache, P. (2023). Adaptive learning using artificial intelligence in e-learning: A literature review. *Education Sciences,* 13(12), 1216.https://doi.org/10.3390/educsci13121216

Gocen, A., & Aydemir, F. (2020).Artificial Intelligence in Education and Schools. Research on Education and Media, 12(1), 13–21. https://doi.org/10.2478/REM-2020-0003.

Jaili, S., Dayo, F., Jun, G., Shuangyao, L., & Najam, S. (2024). The Impact of Artificial Intelligence on Personalized Learning in Education: A Systematic Review. Pak. J. life soc. Science, 22(2), 7412-7428.

Jiang C, Pang Y (2023). Enhancing design thinking in engineering students with project-based learning. *Computer Applications in Engineering Education, n/a(n/a).* https://doi.org/10.1002/cae.22608.

Marino-Campos, C. (2025). The impact of artificial intelligence on personalized learning in higher education A systematic review. *Trend in higher education,* 4(17).

Seo, K., Tang, J., Roll, I., Fels, S., & Yoon, D. (2021). The impact of artificial intelligence on learner–instructor interaction in online learning. *International Journal of Educational Technology in Higher Education*, 18(1), 1–23. https://doi.org/10.1186/S41239-021-00292-9/TABLES/7.

Yigci, D.; Eryilmaz, M.; Yetisen, A.K.; Tasoglu, S.; Ozcan, A. (2024).Large Language Model-Based Chatbots in Higher Education. *Adv. Intell. Syst.*, 7.

15

AI-Powered Adaptive Learning System: Efficacy and Limitations

Md. Faruk Ahmed

Assistant Professor, Department of Business Administration
Girijananda Chowdhury University, Assam
Email: farukahmed385@gmail.com

Abstract

Artificial Intelligence (AI) is revolutionizing the learning environment by making adaptive learning systems a possibility that individualizes instruction, tracks learner progress in real time and caters to varied learning needs. Through this research paper, the effectiveness and shortcomings of AI-driven adaptive learning systems, together with their impact on learner engagement, academic outcomes, and teaching strategies are discussed. The research applies a qualitative-descriptive approach, combining findings from Indian and international literature, actual case studies and policy reports to provide an integrated analysis. The results reveal that adaptive learning systems hugely enhance learning outcomes through tailored feedback, real-time content calibration and data-driven intelligence, helping students in K–12, higher education and corporate learning. Teachers are increasingly set to function as facilitators and interpreters of AI-produced information, needing new skills in data literacy and educational technology. Nonetheless, a number of challenges remain among them are algorithmic bias, privacy, transparency, the digital divide and the limited ability of AI to handle emotional and social aspects of learning. In addition, greater ethical policy frameworks, teacher-AI collaboration models and inclusive infrastructure are needed. The article also discusses future directions, including integrating affective computing, VR/AR, multimodal analytics and creating open-source and localized adaptive platforms. These technologies promise more empathetic, immersive and inclusive learning spaces. The research concludes by suggesting a balanced and human-focused approach to integrating AI in such a manner that technology supports and does not replace the teacher's role in endowing students with holistic learning.

Keywords: *Artificial Intelligence (AI), Adaptive Learning Systems, Learner Engagement, Educational Technology, Algorithmic Bias, Personalized Learning, Affective Computing*

Introduction

The educational landscape is seeing a major shift with the integration of Artificial Intelligence (AI), most prominently with regard to adaptive learning. Adaptive learning systems powered by AI tailor content and pace of learning according to individual learner profiles, hence optimizing outcomes. These systems utilize algorithms, machine learning, and big data analytics to track student performance in real-time and dynamically modify instruction to meet varied learning needs, styles, and rates. Consequently, AI is not only streamlining education processes but also transforming pedagogy by making decisions based on data and learner-centred instruction. In India, with classrooms tending to have high teacher-to-student ratios and heterogeneous learning backgrounds, adaptive learning systems based on AI hold great promise. EdTech firms and organizations are more and more investing in smart platforms that have the potential to deliver scalable, equitable, and personalized learning experiences. Byju's, Embibe, and Toppr are some tools that have already embedded adaptive AI systems into their products, showcasing enhanced student engagement and performance. Yet, the actual effectiveness of such systems is still an object of intense criticism. Concerns about their educational validity, sustained intellectual effects, and compatibility with curriculum guidelines should be more closely examined.

Meanwhile, the limitations of AI-driven adaptive learning systems must not be ignored. They are algorithmic bias, privacy, lack of transparency in AI decision-making, and the digital divide that can widen existing disparities in access to quality education. Further, excessive dependence on automation is causing concern regarding the erosion of the human teacher's role and emotional intelligence in the teaching-learning process. The purpose of this research paper is to study the dual nature of AI-based adaptive learning systems by considering both their effectiveness and inherent limitation. Analysing Indian academic literature and actual implementations, the paper endeavours to address the key questions on how such systems can be optimized for maximum educationally beneficial outcomes while solving ethical, technological, and pedagogical challenges. Overall, the research adds to the debate on the future of education in an AI-based world, particularly in the socio-educational paradigm in India.

Research Methodology

This study uses a qualitative-descriptive approach to examine the efficacy and challenges of AI-powered adaptive learning across educational contexts. Relying on secondary data from journals, reports, and case studies of platforms like Knewton, Squirrel AI, Dream Box, and Carnegie Learning, it reviews AI's role in personalized learning, learner outcomes, teacher roles, and ethics. Indian perspectives are highlighted to localize the global discussion. Findings are thematically synthesized to address system effectiveness, challenges, educator roles, and future innovations, offering practical insights for academia, policy, and EdTech development.

Objectives of the Study

1. To evaluate the efficacy of AI-powered adaptive learning systems in improving student performance by way of identifying and analysing the key challenges and limitations associated.
2. To examine real-world case studies and investigate future directions and technological innovations related to adaptive learning systems.

Literature Reviews

Mangal & Mangal (2021): AI enables personalized pacing, real-time feedback, and content scaffolding, helping bridge gaps between learner ability and achievement.

Pillai & Ranjan (2020): AI-driven adaptive systems improved retention and motivation in Indian classrooms, though lack of teacher training hindered adoption.

Mehta & Gupta (2019): Students using adaptive platforms scored higher than peers in traditional settings; authors caution against tech overreliance without pedagogy.

Bansal & Joshi (2022): In higher education, AI reduces dropouts and personalizes content but raises concerns over data privacy and consent.

Sharma (2020): The success of adaptive AI depends heavily on data quality and diversity, a challenge in India's multilingual context.

Singh &Verma (2021): Adaptive AI boosted critical thinking more than standard e-learning, but rural learners faced tech access issues.

Kumar & Das (2018): AI pilot programs in government schools reduced learning gaps; authors stress need for supportive policy frameworks.

Chakraborty (2019): Platforms like Embibe and Toppr excel in test prep, but algorithmic opacity limits transparency for users.

Reddy & Iyer (2020): AI eased complex learning in engineering education, though lack of multilingual support limited reach.

Patil & Deshmukh (2021): AI increased engagement in Maharashtra schools; study recommends blended learning to retain teacher roles.

Banerjee (2022): Ethical concerns raised over surveillance and commercialization in adaptive systems due to weak regulation.

Khan & Yadav (2023): AI supports NEP 2020's competency-based goals, but teacher empowerment remains key to effective implementation.

Efficacy of AI-Powered Adaptive Learning Systems

1. Enhanced Learner Performance and Engagement: Adaptive systems driven by AI enhance learner performance and engagement through personalization of content to every learner's ability and speed, bridging learning gaps. Research such as Mehta & Gupta (2019) in Indian schools indicates improved test results among learners using these platforms. Interactivity, instant feedback, and gamification also enhance motivation and dropout rates, engaging learners through difficult subjects.

2. Personalization in Real-Time: Adaptive systems constantly observe learners' responses and behaviour, changing content in real time. Underperforming students receive additional help, while high-achieving students may proceed more quickly. Dynamic personalization precludes boredom and frustration, making a major contribution to more efficient learning and greater insight.

3. Accommodation of Varied Learning Styles and Paces: Adaptive systems accommodate various learning styles visual, auditory, or kinesthetics through varied content formats such as videos, quizzes, and simulations. Learners learn at their own pace, and this helps especially those with varying backgrounds, learning difficulties, or language limitations, making these systems extremely efficient in India's diverse classrooms.

4. Improved Teacher Insights Through Analytics: AI platforms give educators comprehensive analytics on student achievement, participation, and areas of weakness. Dashboards point out which students require assistance and what subjects need attention, making teachers facilitators and coaches. In high student-to-teacher ratios in countries such as India, such information assists in directing interventions and better coping with heavy class loads.

5. Use Cases Across K-12, Higher Education, and Corporate Training: In K-12, learning pathways are tailored for individual students by platforms such as BYJU'S and Toppr. Adaptive tools in higher education institutions are used for blended learning and self-paced learning, particularly in subjects that are difficult to learn. In corporate training, AI-powered systems tailor learning modules, accelerate training, and enhance knowledge retention, ensuring effective learning across industries.

6. Evidence from Empirical Studies and Real-World Implementations: Several studies validate the advantages of adaptive learning. Kumar & Das (2018) identified better performance in rural Indian schools, and Singh & Verma (2021) observed enhanced critical thinking in undergraduates with adaptive instruments. Across the world, Carnegie Learning registered a 30% improvement in math scores, and IBM reported up to 60% less training time with AI-based corporate adaptive learning systems.

Challenges in AI-Powered Adaptive Learning Systems

1. Algorithmic Bias: *Reinforcement of Stereotypes and Discrimination*: Many AI systems carry biases inherited from past data, with the potential for unfair judgments or content suggestions for marginalized populations. In India's multicultural society, such bias has the potential to exacerbate educational disparities, restricting access and eroding students' confidence, particularly among underrepresented groups.

2. Data Privacy and Security: *Concerns Over Student Data Usage*: Adaptive platforms harvest sensitive information on students' performance and behaviour, triggering serious privacy threats. Inadequate data protection legislation, especially in

India, increases risks of invasion or exploitation. Students, as well as parents, tend to be unclear about how data is stored and transferred, which creates ethical issues.

3. Lack of Transparency in Decision-Making (Black-Box AI): Most adaptive systems are "black boxes," which it is difficult for teachers or students to comprehend or question AI-based suggestions. This lack of transparency lowers confidence, inhibits error correction, and restricts authentic human-AI interaction in learning environments.

4. Limited Emotional and Social Intelligence: *Difficulty Understanding Affective States*: Whereas AI is good at evaluating academic proficiency and progress, it has not been able to identify emotional expressions such as boredom or stress. AI is not empathetic and sensitive like human teachers, which presents a major disadvantage in emotionally charged learning contexts such as those in India.

5. Digital Divide: *Disparity in Access to Technology and Internet*: Widespread absence of digital equipment, internet penetration, and digital literacy continues to exclude numerous learners from AI-enhanced learning. In India, digital exclusion ranges from rural communities to girls, and low-income communities, threatening greater educational disparities.

6. Over-Reliance on Automation: *Lower Human Engagement in Teaching*: Over-reliance on automated systems may relegate the teachers' role as guides and mentors into the background. While AI performs mundane tasks, human touch, ethical advice, or learning through teamwork cannot be substituted by AI, which are indispensable for well-rounded development and thinking critically.

7. Context Insensitivity: *AI Unable to Adapt to Socio-Cultural Learning Environments* Most adaptive systems are designed with universal models that are oblivious to local cultures, languages, and curricula. In India, context insensitivity of such AI tools renders them less effective for regional-medium students, opposing actual personalization and inclusivity within diverse learning environments.

Case Studies on AI-Powered Adaptive Learning Systems

The global education landscape has seen a surge in the development and deployment of AI-powered adaptive learning systems. These platforms are being integrated into K–12 classrooms, higher education and corporate training environments. By analysing some of the most prominent platforms including Knewton, Squirrel AI, Dream Box Learning and Carnegie Learning we can better understand both the potential and the practical challenges associated with adaptive learning systems.

1. Knewton (Pearson) – United States

Knewton, since acquired by Pearson, was among the original big-ticket adaptive learning platforms. Its aim was to make learning more personalized by tracking learner's behaviour and providing content targeted to them in real-time. It had mastery assessment in real time, dynamic adjustments to instruction, and integration with textbooks and online courses. Trials proved it increased course completion and participation in college-level math and science. But it was criticized for lack of transparency in its algorithms, scalability issues, and compatibility problems with conventional teaching. It was eventually restructured under Pearson due to limited adoption after pilots.

Source: *Business Wire. (2013, November 5). Knewton and Arizona State University partner to improve student achievement in developmental math.*

2. Squirrel AI – China

Squirrel AI, the top Chinese EdTech firm, established adaptive learning with cutting-edge AI. It adapts the teaching of such subjects as math and science, monitoring thousands of micro-concepts per learner to provide customized tutoring. Diagnostic tests create cognitive profiles for every student. Studies recorded gains in learning efficiency of 30–50%, including success in low-resource schools, such as a rural Chinese school that saw a boost in national examination scores. Challenges still exist, including high costs, narrow reach outside city limits, and data privacy concerns and substituting teachers with machines.

Source: *The Guardian. (2019, December 26). Inside China's classrooms: The rise of AI teaching assistants.*

3. Dream Box Learning – United States

Dream Box Learning is a leading K–8 adaptive math platform in the United States, modulating content and feedback on the basis of the way students works through problems, not merely correct solutions. It provides real-time adaptability and teacher dashboards with actionable feedback. Curriculum-aligned, Dream Box has demonstrated solid results; a Harvard study has reported that 60 minutes of weekly work could greatly improve math performance, particularly for struggling learners and English language learners. In Howard County, Maryland, it closed achievement gaps. Nevertheless, teachers found it difficult to incorporate its insights, and there is worry about overdependence diminishing teacher-directed instruction.

Source: *Centre for Education Policy Research at Harvard University. (2019). The impact of Dream Box Learning on student achievement.*

4. Carnegie Learning – United States

Carnegie Learning, designed at Carnegie Mellon University, pairs adaptive software with teacher-supported instruction in math and reading. Its MATHia platform applies cognitive science to mimic one-on-one tutoring, providing real-time feedback and analysis of errors. A U.S. Department of Education study revealed students who used Carnegie Learning made higher gains than conventional methods, increasing problem-solving and critical thinking capabilities. Schools in Kentucky and Texas noticed increased test scores and decreased dropouts when they started using MATHia. However, it all hinged on the teacher's preparation and guidance, and some students just didn't like the interface as much as more modern gamified applications.

Source: *Business Wire. (2021, October 14). Carnegie Learning research shows gains in Algebra I.*

Synthesis of Key Findings

Platform	*Positive Outcomes*	*Challenges*
Knewton	Improved completion rates; personalized learning	Algorithm transparency; scalability
Squirrel AI	Increased learning efficiency; rural school improvement	Cost; data ethics; cultural sensitivity
Dream Box Learning	Math achievement gains; inclusivity	Integration with curricula; risk of reduced teacher input
Carnegie Learning	Boosted critical thinking; effective blended model	Technical rigidity; need for teacher training

Role of Educators in AI-Powered Adaptive Systems

Although AI-driven adaptive learning platforms are proactive in providing personalized instruction and instant feedback, they cannot replace the humane approach to learning. Teachers cannot be eliminated but continue to be important facilitators, mentors, motivators, and interpreters of AI insights. As learning becomes more technology-oriented, the role of the educator has to be reshaped and consolidated—not diminished.

1. Teachers as Facilitators and Interpreters of AI Insights: Adaptive systems create rich information about student performance, but it's educators who translate and use these findings in a meaningful way. Educators identify learning deficits, provide individualized academic and emotional help, modify teaching approaches, and ensure AI results are equitable and pertinent. Educators interpret sophisticated analytics as classroom actions with bearing on actual educational objectives.

2. Significance of Human Interaction, Mentorship, and Inspiration: AI does not have emotional intelligence and is unable to replace the genuine mentorship, inspiration, and moral support of educators. Teachers foster motivation, model empathy and grit, and facilitate social-emotional learning among students. They also develop collaboration, resolve conflicts, and establish trust—key aspects of a supportive and productive learning environment.

3. Teacher Training in EdTech Tools and Data Literacy: For successful AI integration, educators must be trained in digital technology and data analysis. This involves learning adaptive tools, reading student data, and integrating insight into lesson planning. Professional continuous development, backed by schools and governments, is necessary particularly in underfunded schools to enhance teacher confidence and capability with EdTech.

4. Re-imagining the Teacher's Role in a Data-Driven Classroom: While AI performs mundane work such as grading, teachers become strategic leaders—curating learning experience, mentoring students, and making data-driven choices. Instead of being replaced, teachers ought to be working with AI, co-creating education tools, and making sure that technology enhances pedagogy, equity, and student well-being.

Future Directions of AI-Powered Adaptive Learning Systems:

The potential of AI-based adaptive learning is to develop systems that are not merely personalized but also empathetic, engaging, and inclusive. Emotional AI or affective computing will enable platforms to recognize and respond to the emotions of learners—such as boredom, confusion, or frustration—through facial expression, voice, and behaviour, allowing for timely intervention and more human-like interaction. VR and AR integration will offer immersive, real-time adaptive experiences like virtual labs or historical restaging, maximizing interactivity and learning retention. Multimodal learning analytics will personalize further by analysing a combination of text, speech, and visual cues to gain a better understanding of each learner's requirements. Open-source adaptive platforms can open the door to equity, particularly in under-resourced environments, by allowing customization and minimizing costs. In addition, AI-driven localization will make content culturally appropriate and linguistically viable, especially in multilingual and rural areas such as India. All of these innovations together can assure adaptive learning becomes more equitable, emotionally intelligent, and effective across different educational terrain.

Conclusion

In conclusion, AI-powered adaptive learning systems present transformative opportunities for personalized, data-driven, and inclusive education. They enhance learner performance, support diverse needs, and empower educators with actionable insights. However, their full potential is limited by challenges such as algorithmic bias, privacy concerns, lack of emotional intelligence, and digital inequity. Future advancements in affective computing, VR/AR, and open-source platforms hold promise for more empathetic and accessible learning. To ensure ethical and effective implementation, a balanced, human-centric approach is essential—where educators remain central to fostering meaningful learning experiences in collaboration with intelligent systems.

References

Banerjee, D. (2022). Ethical dilemmas in AI-enabled adaptive education. *Indian Journal of Ethics in Education*, *5*(1), 11–20.

Bansal, A., & Joshi, N. (2022). AI in higher education: A study on personalization and privacy. *Journal of Learning Technologies in Higher Education*, *14*(3), 55–63.

Chakraborty, P. (2019). Analysing adaptive learning platforms in India: Promise and pitfalls. *Journal of Emerging Technologies in Education*, *7*(3), 29–38.

Khan, M., & Yadav, P. (2023). The role of AI in implementing NEP 2020: A case for adaptive learning. *Journal of Indian Educational Reform*, *15*(1), 73–82.

Kumar, V., & Das, S. (2018). Adaptive learning in Indian government schools: Challenges and opportunities. *Educational Policy Review India*, *6*(2), 19–27.

Mangal, S. K., & Mangal, U. (2021).*Digital learning and the role of AI in education*. New Delhi: Arya Publications.

Mehta, P., & Gupta, A. (2019).Evaluating adaptive AI platforms in secondary education. *Indian Journal of Educational Research and Technology*, *9*(1), 22–30.

Patil, M., & Deshmukh, S. (2021).Impact of AI-based adaptive learning in Maharashtra schools. *Indian Journal of School Education Technology*, *13*(2), 59–66.

Pillai, R., & Ranjan, R. (2020). Smart learning environments in Indian classrooms: A study on AI-powered adaptive systems. *International Journal of Educational Technology and Learning*, *10*(2), 45–53.

Reddy, K., & Iyer, S. (2020). AI-powered adaptive systems in engineering education: Effectiveness and limitations. *Journal of Engineering Pedagogy in India*, *12*(1), 41–49.

Sharma, R. (2020). A critical review of EdTech platforms and AI in Indian education. *Journal of Digital Pedagogies*, *8*(2), 34–42.

Singh, A., &Verma, R. (2021).Comparative impact of AI-based and traditional learning systems on student critical thinking. *Indian Journal of Educational Innovation*, *11*(4), 67–76.

16

The Ethics and Challenges of AI in Education

Geyin Miyu[1] & Tongmak Dada[2]

[1]PhD Scholar, Department of Education. Rajiv Gandhi University, Doimukh
[2]PhD Scholar, Dept. of Mass Communication, Rajiv Gandhi University, Doimukh
Email: geyinmiyu18@gmail.com

Abstract

Artificial intelligence (AI) is transforming the world of education, offering new possibilities for enhancing teaching and learning, personalizing instruction, improving assessment, and increasing access and equity. AI does hold potential if used wisely like in a deeply unequal society, AI tools can offer students from less privileged backgrounds access to explanations, resources, and support they wouldn't otherwise get. AI won't erase inequality, but it can offer opportunity based on curiosity and ability, not just privilege. However, AI also poses significant ethical challenges that need to be carefully considered and addressed by educators, policymakers, researchers, and developers. Today, the fear isn't about Google anymore. It's about AI, digital classrooms, and how technology is reshaping education. What is the future of learning in a world where AI evolves rapidly and knowledge is freely available online? Can digital education replace classrooms, or should it only support them? The main focus of this paper is to discuss the ethics and challenges of AI in Education and to forecast some possible solutions to the issues relating AI in Education.

Keywords: *Artificial Intelligence (AI), ethics, challenges, Education.*

Introduction

We may not think about artificial intelligence (AI) on a daily basis, but it is all around us, and we have been using it for years. When we are doing a Google search, reading our emails, getting a doctor's appointment, asking for driving directions, or getting movie and music recommendations, we are constantly using the applications of AI and its assistance in our lives. This need for assistance and our dependence on AI systems has become even more apparent during the COVID-19 pandemic. The growing impact and dominance of AI systems reveals itself in healthcare, education, communications, transportation, agriculture, and more. It is almost impossible to live in a modern society without encountering applications powered by AI.

The term "artificial intelligence" was actually coined in 1956. In that year, John McCarthy, a Dartmouth College professor, organized a pivotal workshop that coined the term "artificial intelligence" and aimed to create machines capable of reasoning and using human language. After a fast start, research interest in AI cooled for a few decades before developments in computer technology drove a resurgence in the 1990s with advances in machine learning and neural networks. The public release of Chat GPT in 2022 marked a significant milestone, showcasing unprecedented capabilities in natural language understanding and generation, and fueling further advancements in AI. Today, AI significantly impacts various sectors, from healthcare to finance, manufacturing, and transportation. Many think it is also poised to revolutionize education.

Artificial Intelligence (AI) has the potential to address some of the biggest challenges in education today, innovate teaching and learning practices, and accelerate progress towards SDG. However, rapid technological developments inevitably bring multiple risks and challenges, which have so far outpaced policy debates and regulatory frameworks. UNESCO is committed to supporting Member States to harness the potential of AI technologies for achieving the Education 2030 Agenda, while ensuring that its application in educational contexts is guided by the core principles of inclusion and equity. UNESCO's mandate calls inherently for a human-centred approach to AI. It aims to shift the conversation to include AI's role in addressing current inequalities regarding access to knowledge, research and the diversity of cultural expressions and to ensure AI does not widen the technological divides within and between countries. The promise of "AI for all" must be that everyone can take advantage of the technological revolution under way and access its fruits, notably in terms of innovation and knowledge.

Within the framework of the Beijing Consensus, UNESCO developed Artificial intelligence and education: Guidance for policy-makers to foster the readiness of education policy-makers in artificial intelligence. It aims to generate a shared understanding of the opportunities and challenges that AI offers for education, as well as its implications for the core competencies needed in the AI era. UNESCO also published AI competency frameworks for students and teachers to guide countries in supporting students and teachers to understand the potential as well as risks of AI.

Like so many of the technologies that have changed the world, artificial intelligence (AI) developed over many years before it seemed to suddenly burst on the scene. Today, AI is ubiquitous and offers revolutionary potential for education. With AI, educators can tailor learning experiences to individual student needs, making education more effective and engaging. AI-enabled technologies also assist in administrative tasks, streamlining operations and freeing up educators to focus on teaching. Learn more about how teachers and school administrators are using AI-powered tools today and the possibilities for the future of artificial intelligence in education.

Computer-assisted instruction (CAI) began in the 1960s, presenting instructional material with expensive mainframe computers. As computer technology became smaller and more affordable, more schools were able to adopt CAI. Intelligent tutoring systems emerged with the advent of desktop computers, offering tutorial programs that provided immediate feedback and tailored learning paths based on student responses. These systems demonstrated the potential benefits of personalized learning, making technology adoption in education increasingly attractive. The widespread adoption of AI in the last few years, including its growing use in schools, has caused reactions ranging from outright banning to enthusiastic embrace. Because the tools will continue to evolve and change the way we operate in all areas of life, teachers and educational administrators need to come to terms with several ethical considerations about AI in education.

Government of India's New Education Policy (NEP) 2020 emphasizes the integration of AI curriculum at all educational levels and aims to equip students with skills like digital literacy, coding and computational thinking. CBSE introduced AI as a subject for students in classes IX to XII, and has also partnered with IBM to launch the Skills Build Program, which includes orientation sessions on generative AI. In collaboration with Intel, CBSE has also developed an AI Facilitator Handbook which provides educators with comprehensive training materials and real-life examples. From the 2025-26 sessions, the CISCE board has introduced robotics and AI as part of its curriculum. AI/GenAI features prominently in the curriculum of India's top business schools, including the IIMs and ISB. And Country like China is making substantial investments and offering tax incentives and other motivators, in tools like the adaptive tutoring platform Squirrel AI which leverage extensive datasets and camera surveillance to enhance performance on standardized tests. Finland has taken a bold national step towards AI-driven education by providing free online coursework for its citizens. Approximately 50% of schools have adopted the ViLLE platform, which offers instant feedback and analytical insights on student assignments to both students and teachers. South Korea is making significant investments in the education of its students. The country's goal is to incorporate AI coursework into its national curriculum at all grade levels, with the initiative set to begin at the high school level by 2025. Singapore is a leader in the use of technology in education. The government has invested heavily in AI for education and Singaporean schools and universities use GenAI extensively.

Artificial Intelligence (AI) is no longer a futuristic concept; it is now a transformative force reshaping various industries, including education. AI's integration into educational systems promises to enhance learning experiences, streamline administrative processes, and personalize education for students worldwide. This blog explores the current trends in AI in education and examines the future implications of these technological advancements. The role of AI in education is rapidly expanding, offering transformative trends that enhance learning experiences and improve educational outcomes. As we look to the future, the potential implications of AI in education are vast, promising a more personalized, accessible, and efficient educational landscape. However, it is crucial to address ethical considerations and ensure data privacy to harness the full potential of AI in a responsible and equitable manner. The future of education is being shaped by AI, and its impact will be felt for generations to come. As educators, students, and policymakers navigate this evolving landscape, embracing the opportunities and challenges presented by AI will be key to realizing its transformative potential in education.

Transformative Impact of AI on Education

The integration of AI in education is transforming the way students learn and educators teach. Here are some of the key impacts:

1. Enhanced Learning Experiences: AI provides interactive and engaging learning experiences through personalized content, intelligent tutoring, and immersive technologies like virtual and augmented reality. Learners are no longer required to invest extensive hours in searching for information they can effortlessly input a command or pose a question, and artificial intelligence provides the information instantaneously. This not only conserves time but also enhances efficiency by delivering prompt feedback and focused assistance.

2. Improved Accessibility: AI-powered tools can accommodate diverse learning needs, making education more inclusive. For example, speech recognition software and AI- driven language translation tools assist students with disabilities by providing instant captions, real-time subtitles, and sign language interfaces. These tools also support students learning in non-native languages by translating content into multiple languages, helping them learn in their native tongue. All of this contributes to making education more flexible, inclusive, and accessible for everyone.

3. Efficiency in Administration: AI automates administrative tasks such as grading, scheduling, and attendance tracking, allowing educators to focus more on teaching and student support. From the admissions process to evaluations, artificial intelligence assists administrative personnel by alleviating their workload, allowing both educators and administrators to detect issues at an early stage and offer prompt assistance.

4. Data-Driven Decision Making: AI enables educators to make informed decisions based on real-time data analytics. By understanding student performance trends, educators can implement targeted interventions and improve educational outcomes. Artificial Intelligence tools can assist in the analysis of students' test scores and their participation levels, enabling the identification of students who require additional support from educators, as well as determining the most suitable teaching methods for those needing extra attention.

Current Trends in AI in Education:

Artificial Intelligence (AI) represents a sophisticated technology that allows machines to emulate human thought processes, learning abilities, and decision-making skills. It is revolutionizing the educational landscape, with AI being regarded as the technology of the future that will augment human potential in numerous domains. "In the future, intelligent machines will either supplant or enhance human abilities across various fields. Artificial Intelligence has emerged as a prominent focus within computer science, markedly enhancing productivity in manufacturing, services, and education over the last twenty years. The emergence of expert systems, AI-driven technologies designed to tackle intricate problems—has resulted in improved quality and efficiency in multiple sectors." (Thakur &Kaur, 2023). AI is being utilized in diverse ways within the educational landscape. Here are some of the most notable trends:

1. Personalized Learning: AI algorithms analyze students' learning habits, strengths, and weaknesses to tailor educational content to individual needs. DreamBox and Knewton both educational technology platforms that offer adaptive learning experiences, providing customized lessons that evolve as students' progress. DreamBox focuses on providing interactive and math instruction specifically from kindergarten to class 8th whereas Knewton offers a broader platform that integrates with various educational resources and used across different subjects and grade level.

2. Intelligent Tutoring Systems: AI-powered tutoring systems, such as Carnegie Learning and Squirrel both companies focused on using AI and provide personalized instruction and feedback to students. These systems can identify areas where students struggle and offer targeted interventions to help them improve. Carnegie Learning is a US-based company known for its AI-powered math software and curriculum, while Squirrel AI is a Chinese company that provides AI-driven adaptive learning across various subjects.

3. Automated Grading and Assessment: AI is streamlining the grading process by automating the assessment of assignments and exams. Grade scope is an American ed-tech company that offers online and AI-assisted grading tools for higher education. Founded in 2014. It use machine learning to grade written responses, saving educator's time and providing consistent, objective evaluations.

4. Natural Language Processing (NLP): Natural Language Processing (NLP) technologies, including chatbots which is a computer programs created to mimic human dialogue through text or voice interactions—and virtual assistants, enhance communication between students and educators. AI-powered platforms such as Duolingo and Coursera utilize NLP to engage with learners, respond to their inquiries, and offer immediate assistance.

5. Data Analytics: AI-powered data analytics tools assist educators in tracking student performance, recognizing students who may be at risk, and formulating targeted intervention strategies. For instance, BrightBytes, a company specializing in learning analytics, integrates data with educational research to enhance and assess learning outcomes. Additionally, Civitas provides actionable analytics through AI-driven workflows, enabling higher education institutions to make informed decisions, collaborate effectively, and expand proactive support.

Future Implications of AI in Education

As AI continues to evolve, its implications for the future of education are profound. Here are some potential future developments:

1. **Lifelong Learning and Continuous Education**: AI will facilitate lifelong learning by providing personalized, on-demand educational resources. Individuals will be able to upskill and reskill throughout their careers,

adapting to the changing job market. Later it will led to development of skill in every individual which will help them throughout their career or lifetime.

2. **Global Education Equity**: AI has the potential to bridge educational gaps by providing quality education to underserved and remote areas. As there are still so many citizens that are deprived of Education and with proper development of AI in Education can bridge those gaps. AI-driven platforms can offer scalable and affordable learning solutions to students worldwide which makes easy for them to access education throughout the system.
3. **Ethical and Privacy Considerations**: AI systems rely heavily on data, often including personal information like browsing habits, location data and even biometric identifiers. And without proper safeguards, this data could be misused, leading to serious consequences for individuals and organizations. As AI becomes more integrated into education, addressing ethical concerns and ensuring data privacy will be paramount. Developing robust policies and practices to protect student information and promote ethical AI use is essential.
4. **Evolving Roles of Educators**: The role of educators will shift as AI takes on more administrative and instructional tasks. Educators will become facilitators of learning from a knowledge disseminator, focusing on mentorship, critical thinking, and social-emotional development. AI tools will handle routine tasks, allowing teachers to focus on building relationships, inspiring curiosity and guiding students towards success.
5. **Interdisciplinary Learning**: Interdisciplinary learning involves integrating knowledge and methods from different academic fields to address complex problems or explore a topic from multiple perspectives. AI will promote interdisciplinary learning by integrating knowledge from various fields. Students will engage in project-based learning that combines science, technology, engineering, arts, and mathematics (STEAM), fostering creativity and innovation. It encourages students to make connections between subjects, fostering a deeper understanding and developing critical thinking, problem solving and creativity

The Ethics and challenges of AI in Education:

AI in education can raise various ethical issues, such as:

1. **Bias and discrimination**: AI systems may reflect or amplify human biases and prejudices, leading to unfair or discriminatory outcomes for certain groups of students or teachers. For example, AI systems may use data that is incomplete, inaccurate, or unrepresentative of the diversity of learners, or they may apply algorithms that are not transparent or accountable for their decisions.
2. **Privacy and data protection**: AI systems may collect, store, process, and share large amounts of personal and sensitive data from students and teachers, such

as academic performance, behaviour, preferences, emotions, biometrics, or health information. This may pose risks to their privacy and data protection rights, especially if the data is used for purposes other than education, such as commercialization, surveillance, or profiling.

3. **Autonomy and agency**: AI systems may influence or interfere with the autonomy and agency of students and teachers, affecting their ability to make informed choices, exercise control over their learning processes, express their creativity, or develop critical thinking skills. For example, AI systems may provide recommendations or feedback that are not aligned with the learners' goals, interests, or values, or they may replace human interaction and guidance with automated responses.
4. **Transparency and explain ability**: AI systems may operate in opaque or complex ways that are difficult to understand or question by students, teachers, or other stakeholders. This may limit their ability to trust, verify, challenge, or appeal the actions or outcomes of AI systems. For example, AI systems may use black-box algorithms that do not reveal how they reach their conclusions or predictions.
5. **Accountability and responsibility**: AI systems may raise questions about who is accountable or responsible for their design, development, deployment, use, or impact in education. This may create gaps or ambiguities in the allocation of roles and duties among different actors involved in the AI ecosystem. For example, AI systems may cause harm or errors that are not attributable to any specific human agent.
6. **Over-reliance:** One of the main concerns about the adoption of generative AI is the risk of becoming too dependent on this technology. In essence, it's the same debate as whether or to what extent calculators, computers, or smartphones should be allowed in the classroom.

Why is it important to address the ethical issues of AI in education?

Addressing the ethical issues of AI in education is important for several reasons:

1. To protect human rights and dignity: The ethical issues of AI in education may affect the fundamental human rights and dignity of students and teachers. For example,

- Bias and discrimination may violate the right to education without discrimination
- Privacy and data protection may violate the right to privacy
- Autonomy and agency may violate the right to freedom of thought
- Transparency and explain ability may violate the right to information
- Accountability and responsibility may violate the right to remedy

2. To ensure quality and effectiveness: The ethical issues of AI in education may affect the quality and effectiveness of educational processes and outcomes. For example,

- Bias and discrimination may reduce the accuracy and validity of assessment
- Privacy and data protection may undermine the trust and confidence of learners
- Autonomy and agency may hinder the motivation and engagement of learners
- Transparency and explain ability may impair the feedback and guidance of learners
- Accountability and responsibility may compromise the evaluation and improvement of learning

3. To foster inclusion and equity: The ethical issues of AI in education may affect the inclusion and equity of educational opportunities and benefits. For example,

- Bias and discrimination may exacerbate existing inequalities and marginalization
- Privacy and data protection may expose vulnerable groups to exploitation or harm
- Autonomy and agency may limit the participation and empowerment of learners
- Transparency and explain ability may create information asymmetries or gaps
- Accountability and responsibility may shift the burden or blame to learners

How can we address the ethical issues of AI in education?

Addressing the ethical issues of AI in education requires a multi-stakeholder approach that involves collaboration among educators, policymakers, researchers, developers, and other factors in the AI ecosystem. Some of the possible actions that can be taken are:

- **Developing ethical frameworks and guidelines**: Ethical frameworks and guidelines can provide a common vision and a set of principles and values to guide the ethical design, development, deployment, use, and impact of AI in education. For example, UNESCO has published the first-ever global standard on AI ethics – the 'Recommendation on the Ethics of Artificial Intelligence' in November 2021.
- **Implementing ethical practices and standards**: Ethical practices and standards can operationalize the ethical frameworks and guidelines into concrete actions and measures to ensure the ethical performance and behavior of AI systems in education. For example, ethical practices and standards can include data quality assurance, algorithmic transparency and explain ability, human oversight and intervention, privacy and data protection policies, impact assessment and evaluation, stakeholder participation and consultation, etc.

- **Promoting ethical education and awareness**: Ethical education and awareness can raise the ethical literacy and competence of students, teachers, and other stakeholders in the AI ecosystem. For example, ethical education and awareness can include curriculum integration, professional development, public engagement, media literacy, digital citizenship, etc.
- **Strengthening ethical governance and regulation**: Ethical governance and regulation can provide a legal and institutional framework to ensure the accountability and responsibility of AI factors in education. For example, ethical governance and regulation can include laws and regulations, codes of conduct, ethics committees, oversight bodies, complaint mechanisms, redress mechanisms, etc.
- **Conduct Ethical Impact Assessments:** Before implementing new AI technologies, schools should conduct ethical impact assessments to identify potential risks and benefits, especially for marginalized student populations. This proactive approach helps ensure fairness and avoid unintended consequences.
- **Promote Transparency and Explainability:** Ensure that AI systems used in education are transparent and explainable, allowing users to understand how algorithms work and make informed decisions. This fosters trust and accountability.
- **Prioritize Privacy and Data Security:** Implement robust privacy policies and security measures to protect student data and address concerns about learner privacy. Educators and students should be aware of privacy policies and how their data is being used.
- **Foster Collaboration and Involve Stakeholders:** Include teachers, students, and administrators in the decision-making process regarding AI implementation to ensure buy-in and address concerns. This collaborative approach can help navigate ethical challenges and promote responsible AI use.
- **Share Success Stories and Best Practices:** Highlight examples of successful AI implementations in education and showcase the positive impact on student learning outcomes. This can help alleviate fears and demonstrate the potential of AI in education.
- **Address Bias and Fairness:** Be vigilant about potential biases in AI algorithms and ensure that AI systems used in education are fair and equitable for all students. This includes addressing biases in training data and algorithms.
- **Emphasize Human Oversight:** AI should be used to augment, not replace the role of teachers. Human oversight is crucial for ensuring ethical decision-making and providing personalized learning experiences.
- **Stay Informed and Adapt:** The field of AI is rapidly evolving, so educators and schools should stay informed about new developments and adapt

policies and practices as needed. This ensures that AI is used ethically and responsibly as it continues to evolve.

Conclusion

Artificial intelligence (AI) is a field of study that combines the applications of machine learning, algorithm productions, and natural language processing. Applications of AI transform the tools of education. AI has a variety of educational applications, such as personalized learning platforms to promote students' learning, automated assessment systems to aid teachers, and facial recognition systems to generate insights about learners' behaviors. AI in education offers numerous advantages, including personalised learning experiences, increased efficiency, and enhanced student support and engagement. However, implementing AI in education comes with challenges such as the availability of reliable data and the need for specialised technical expertise. By following best practices, such as starting small, providing training and support, fostering collaboration, and monitoring and evaluating the impact, educators can successfully integrate AI in the classroom.

Generative AI is here to stay and has the potential to revolutionize every sector of the economy, including education. It's up to educators and ed-tech solution providers to determine the most effective way to tap into the technology are potential while mitigating its potential risks.

References

Adams, R., & McIntyre, N. (2020). England A-level downgrades hit pupils from disadvantaged areas hardest.

AI-Powered Learning Analytics Are Shaping Early Childhood Education and Instruction (2023). *Childhood Education International.* The Role of AI In Education: Transformative Trends and Future Implications. *SABEN.*

Akgun, S., & Greenhow, C (2021). Artificial Intelligence in Education: Addressing Ethical challenges in K-12 settings. *National Library of Medicine.*

Ali S. A., et al., (2019). Constructionism, ethics and creativity: developing primary and middle school artificial intelligence education. International Workshop on Education in Artificial Intelligence (EDUAI).

Nguyen, N (2023). Opportunities and challenges of AI in higher education. *FeedbackFruits.* feedbackfruits.com/blog/ opportunities-and-challenges-of-ai-in-higher-education

Patil, N.H et al., (2023). Research Paper on Artificial Intelligence and it's Applications. ResearchGate.

Section IV: Educational Transformations and Emerging Paradigms

17

Good Governance in Assam: Issues, Challenges and Reforms

Dr. Nabanita Baishya

Assistant Professor, Department of Economics, Dhing College, Dhing
Email: nabanita.baishya@gmail.com

Abstract

The concept of "Governance" is not new. It is as old as human civilization .Good governance refers to the ability to deliver goods to the stakeholders. When we talk of good governance, we are referring to the elimination of mal governance and the establishment of good governance through democratic processes and rule of law so that citizens of a country and members of a society do not suffer. It is the purposive and development oriented administration, which concerns the improvement of quality of life of the mass people. It involves government, private sector and people's associations or civil society. Failure to ensure the socio-economic goals is now no longer attributable to the scarcity of resources but to the failure of governance. When the words, "we the people" signify not only the moral and historical insight of founding fathers but they serve to reaffirm they are the source of all constitutional authority and that the test of good governance was measure of people's well-being. However, the functionaries of state have failed to realize that they are servants of the people and not their masters. The main challenge facing the governance process is to build a framework that can promote an appropriate balance between government, private sector and civil society. This paper tries to highlights the main issues and challenges facing in the path of good governance and gives the reforms initiatives taken by various districts of Assam.

Keywords: *Governance, Stakeholders, Democratic Process, Administration, Civil society.*

Introduction

Since independence, the government has been the sole provider of goods and services in several areas. But over the past two decades, many changes are taking place at the global level and these are affecting India also. We have now a strong private sector, which along with the government provides services to the people. Also people's associations or civil society is playing an active role. Presently, we are moving from governing almost exclusively by the formal government to governance, which is broader in nature comprising government, private sector and people's associations and civil society groups. Recently the terms "governance" and "good governance" are being increasingly used in development literature. Ba governance is being increasingly regarded as one of the root causes of all evil within our societies. Major donors and international financial institutions are increasingly banning their aid and loans on the condition that reforms that ensure "good governance" are undertaken. Actually good governance is all about strategic vision, which allows the more knowledge to act within a generally agreed framework coming for result and outcomes. Good governance refers to the ability to deliver goods to the stakeholders. It is purposive and development oriented administration which concerns the improvement of quality of life of the mass people. It involves government, private sector and people's associations on civil society. This paper tries to highlight the main issues and challenges facing in the path of good governance and gives the reforms initiatives taken by various districts of Assam.

Objectives

- This study highlights the major issues and challenges of good governance in Assam.
- To find out the reforms initiatives taken by various districts of Assam.

Methodology

This chapter is basically a descriptive analysis and is based on secondary sources of data.

Concept of Good Governance

Governance in simple terms means the process of decision –making and its implementation in collective problem situation. This does not imply that the efforts of the government earlier were not aimed at effective formulation and implementation of policies. The term 'governance' had become popular especially since 1990s with the usage of the term by international donor agencies such as the World Bank, the United Nations Development Programme (UNDP) etc. The developing countries including India,as we all know, are dependent on the developed countries for technical and financial assistance. These international institutions, for the first time in the beginning of 1990s, drew attention to certain crucial deficiencies in the governance system of the developing countries. These included, non-availability of information to the people, lack of accountability, poor management of the public sector and lack of appropriate legal framework.

Governance emphasizes not just routine implementation of policies and programmes but making the entire activity accountable, democratic, participative and responsive to people's need. Administration in the traditional context has implied formulating and executing policies, within a framework of hierarchy, rules and regulations, citizens being mere passive recipient of services. There is more of formalism in administration than real two way interactions with citizens. Now even the citizens are asserting their rights and demanding better governance.

Good governance refers to the ability to deliver goods to the stakeholders. When we talk of good governance we are referring to the elimination of mal governance and the establishment of good governance through democratic processes and rule of law so that citizens of a country and members of a society do not suffer. It is to make the various agents of political system work for the betterment of all the citizens especially of the marginalized and the vulnerable communities. Good governance is enhancing the ability of the people to gain better and dignified life, greater options to choose from and ensuring transparency in administration etc.

Good governance is ensuring a better today and a brighter future for all the citizens. At one time, the notion of 'govern ability' was also used to discuss the facets of good governance. The concept of govern ability directs attention to a state's capacity to govern. Equally important is the fact that democracy is a remarkably different form of government to create and sustain. The basic principles of good governance are equality, justice, prosperity and democracy. These principles are ensured through participation, decentralization, accountability and transparency. In a developing country like India, governance concerns necessarily have a wide ambit. The recognition that governance takes place in domains other than that of exclusively formal institutionalized political and administrative structures means that governance concerns encompass a variety of spheres. These include the political, economic, the civil society. It is these aspects that would lead to long term sustainability of communities, societies, nations and the universe at large.

Principles of Good Governance:

Good governance is tightly linked to the fight against corruption. Accordingly, some of the core principles of good governance are also principles of anti-corruption. The literature identifies good governance with political systems that are:

1. Participatory
2. Consistent with the rule of law;
3. Transparent;
4. Responsive;
5. Consensus-oriented;
6. Equitable and inclusive;
7. Effective and efficient; and

Accountable (Rothstein and teorel, 2008; UN, (https://www.unescap.org/sites/default /files/good-governance.pdf)

When political systems do not adhere to these eight principles, their institutions might be incapable of delivering public services and fulfill people's needs. The sixth principle is especially worth emphasizing as it ensures that the views of minorities are taken into account and that the voices of the most vulnerable in society are heard in decision-making.

Participatory

Participation by both men and women is a key cornerstone of good governance. Participation could be either direct or through legitimate intermediate institutions or representatives. It is important to point out that representative democracy does not necessarily mean that the concerns of the most vulnerable society would be taken into consideration in decision making. Participation needs to be informed and organized. This means freedom of association and expression on the one hand and an organized civil society on the other hand.

Rule of Law

Good governance requires fair legal frameworks that are enforced impartially. It also requires full protection of human rights, particularly those of minorities. Impartial enforcement of laws requires an independent judiciary and an impartial and incorruptible police force.

Transparent

Transparency means that decisions taken and their enforcement are done in a manner that follows rules and regulations. It also means that information is freely available and directly accessible to those who will be affected by such decisions and their enforcement. It also means that enough information is provided and that it is provided in easily understandable forms and media.

Responsive

Good governance requires that institutions and process try to serve all stakeholders within a reasonable timeframe.

Consensus oriented

There are several factors and as many view points given in a society. Good governance requires meditation of the different interests in society to reach a broad consensus in society on what is in the best interest of the whole community and how this can be achieved. It also requires a broad and long-term perspective on what is needed for sustainable human development and how to achieve the goals of such development. This can only result from an understanding of the historical, cultural and social contexts of a given society or community.

Equitable and inclusive

A society's well-being depends on ensuring that all its members feel that they have a stake in it and do not feel excluded from the mainstream of society. This requires all groups, but particularly the most vulnerable, have opportunities to improve or maintain their well-being.

Effective and efficient

Good governance means that processes and institutions produce results that meet the needs of society while making the best use of resource at their disposal. The concept of efficiency in the context of good governance also covers the sustainable use of natural resources and the protection of the environment.

Accountable

Accountability is a key requirement of good governance. Not only governmental institutions but also the private sector and civil society organizations must be accountable to the public and to their institutional stakeholders. In general an organization or an institution is accountable to those who will be affected by its decisions or actions. Accountability cannot be enforced without transparency and the rule of law.

Major Issues and Challenges:

Governance, as we have discussed occupies an important place in the current administrative scenario. It aims at the maximum welfare of citizens. It involves government, private sector and people' associations or civil society. The important challenge facing the governance process is to build a framework or system that can promote an appropriate balance between these three constituents. The quality of governance is to be improved and sustained.

The important issues and challenges pertaining to governance include:

a. Lack of transparency: One of the major problems of good governance is lack of transparency. It is the duty of the government to make aware of the people regarding plans and programs. Bureaucratic complexities and procedures make it difficult for a citizen as well as the civil society to navigate the system for timely and quality delivery of services. The lack of transparency and secrecy that have been associated with the administrative system from colonial times, besides generating corruption, has also led to injustice and favoritism.

b. Underdevelopment: Underdevelopment is also the challenge of good governance. The fact is that substantial development has flowed into the Assam; its impact on target populations has been negligible because of the corruption and violence of the prevailing politics. Much of this investment, moreover, has indirectly ended up financing militancy through the enveloping economy of extortion and collusion.

c. Threats to peace: The most important public good is the supply of security especially security of life and property. The responsibility of the Indian nation-state to protect their life and property of every citizen is being seriously threatened particularly in areas affected by terrorism (Jammu and Kashmir), insurgency (North-Eastern states), and naxalite violence in 150 districts of India's mainland.

d. Corruption: Corruption is the major problem to Good Governance in Assam. The high level of corruption in Assam has been widely perceived as a major obstacle in improving the quality of governance. The complex and non-transparent system of command and control, monopoly of the government as a service provider, underdeveloped legal framework, and lack of information and weak notion of citizens' rights have been provided incentives for corruption in Assam.

e. Red Tapism: Non-responsiveness on some important issues is also the problem of good governance, Delay in doing work for the people also produced bad governance.

f. Ethnic Conflict: Ethnic conflict also created bad governance. There are many ethnic groups in Assam. But the conflict among them created a disturbed situation in Assam.

New Challenges: The advent of globalization presents a new series of challenges to the administration. Activated by technological improvements, a new inter-national relationship of our interests across issues and boundaries has come into being. Trade and financial developments have tightened to mesh of economic linkages across boundaries and regardless of preferences. The new state of affairs just cannot be wished away but must be engaged with. We should build up expertise to ensure that the interests of our country and the people are not overwhelmed by the force of globalization and that our interests are properly served. Mass political education and raisingof political consciousness become inescapable. This is the task to be performed by political parties. To remain actively involved in new development programs the people would also need the support of well organized, well prepared, knowledge-oriented personnel and well thought out policies. Think tanks and organized intellectual groups would have to be promoted through state funding, etc.

Transparency, public consultation and participation are more important than ever to improve policy and reinforce democracy and stability. Promoting open and transparent government, while guaranteeing security, privacy and civil liberties, is a major challenge of our times. With the proliferation of globalization, we are witnessing the world, where centralizationco-exists with decentralization, independence with interdependence, and sovereign power with supra-national entities. Actually good governance is all about strategic vision, which allow the more knowledgeable to act within a general agreed framework caring for results and outcomes. The 73rd and 74th Constitutional Amendments need to be operatonalised in their real spirit to achieve the objectives of democratic de-centralization, people's participation and economic development. With the passage to Right to Information Act enlightened citizenry has directly entered the arena, which has made the acts of government, pre transparent, responsive and accountable to the people and other stakeholders. The civil society is called upon to ensure god governance and sustainable development at all level. Would the civil society stand up to the test is a milliondollar question.

The attribute of power leads the state or its agencies, at times, to use unwarranted or excessive force or to indulge in some other reprehensible activity. Today public opinion of media are alert enough to compel the state to institute a commission or enquiry in the event of some such act of commission by an official agency. Moreover, for lack of full judicial status to an enquiry commission equivalent to that of a judicial court politicians, officials and other concerned persons do not take the summons and proceedings of the commission with appropriate seriousness deference. An impartial enquiry commission , whenever deem necessary , acts as a healthy check on the arbitrariness and high-handedness of the state and its agencies , provided , of course it completes its findings without avoidable delay and the state is mandatory obligated to act on its findings on a reasonable time-frame. Hopefully, the Constitution can take cognizance of this aspect so that enquiry commissions can become effective tools for initiating corrective or even punitive measures wherever government or administration exceeds its brief.

Reform initiatives by different districts of Assam:

In order to achieve effective integration of the entire governmental machinery, rejuvenation of the system is required. Proper management of human resources is essential for positive transformation of the present system.

As is envisaged in the vision for Assam in 2030, first 2 to 3 years will have to be devoted to put the system into place which will act as a harbinger of change. Professionalism is to be brought to all rank and files to ensure optimum utilization of the human resource and transform it into the agent of change. Without a thoroughly trained and motivated support staff, professionalism in service delivery to the citizens will be very difficult to infuse. With an eye to this training centres at four districts viz, Majuli, Guwahati, Bongaigaon and Silchar are being discussed to cover Grade III and Grade IV employees in all the districts.

Institutional reforms are the core area where drastic steps are to be taken to transform the State Public Service Commission into an institution through which the best and only the best is recruited. Reform in APSC is being taken up to restore public faith in the entire system of recruitment of various Government posts through the commission have been made in this regard and it is felt that it is essential to revamp the examination system in the line of UPSC. Reports of TapanLalBaruah Committee/ MP Bezbaruah Committee and RT Jindal Committee had been published for public view and suggestions and can be taken as the stepping stone forward.

In respect of good governance practices, almost all the districts of Assam have taken reforms initiatives both in the form of offline and online. Since, it is not possible to highlight the reform initiative taken by all the districts, so, in this paper gives the reform measures undertaken by four districts, namely, Kamrup Metro, Jorhat, Goalpara and Hailakandi, which represents both Brahmaputra and Barak Valley.

Kamrup Metropolitan District Administration has taken both offline as well as online activity measures for improvement of good governance. For the quick disposal of day to day works in different branches, disposal of public grievances since 2009, information and Communication Technology Tool,named 'MAHANAGAR, was launched. The following IT Intranet applications are in place right now.

1. Dak Management System
2. File Indexing System insettlement.

3. United Fund Scheme Management System.
4. RTI case disposal system.
5. Help Desk
6. Public Facilitation Centre.
7. Public Petition disposal system.

In respect of online activity, district administration has put in place a web portal kamrupmetroonline.in. A citizen can locate his original registered deed on a click of a mouse and get the document instantly delivered in the Sub Registry Office. A blood donor and information Management System has been included there where a citizen willing to donate blood can register.

Jorhat District Administration has taken some important steps for ensuring good governance, which are as follows,

1. Delegation of various powers and functions to subordinate officers to empower them. Senior officers are not doing those works which should be and can be done at lower level. This has helped senior Management to focus on Priority areas and take strategic decisions for overall development of district.
2. Soft Copy / Scanned copy of all important reports etc. is kept for record and e mail based correspondence is made wherever feasible.
3. New facilities are being provided for general public like newly constructed modern paid toilet, safe drinking water, and public facilitation centre.
4. New SLRM: Solid and Liquid Resource management Centre is being set up in Office Campus to segregate and process Organic and Inorganic waste generated in campus.
5. New Comprehensive Website developed for district administration giving information on all important things about Jorhat and to lodge public grievances, complaints.

Goalpara District Administration has also taken the following important actions regarding implementation of good governance.

1. District administration aims to facilitate the disabled section of the society , with regard to issuing of disability certificate to them. Special camps are organized to diagnose the percentage of disability by specialist doctors.
2. Another initiative has been taken up by Social Welfare and Health department along with the district administration. Administration has taken steps to identify the malnourished children of the district categorise them into moderately malnourished and severely malnourished, ICDS project wise. There are 7 ICDS projects in Goalpara. Camps are held in every project and severely malnourished children are identified. Batch wise, these children are brought to the 'Nutritional Rehabilitation Centre' situated in the civil hospital, Goalpara for providing intense care for a period of 15 days or 30 days as per the requirement.

3. In order to effectively deal with Witching Hunting, it has been directed to constitute village centric vigilance committees consisting of village headman, educated personal, Police, VDP members, Anganwari workers and ASHA, leading citizens and para legal volunteers to nip the crime in the bud and form the first line of defence for the Witch Hunting victims.

Various other reform measures are in the fray for enhancing the good relation between the general public and the administration and to make the offices, people friendly, accessible, transparent and accountable.

In Barak Valley, Hailakandi District Administration has arranged Training on skill development,specially on computer application for quick disposal of office work.

1. ARTPS have been introduced on 55 no. of notified services, D.C. Office, Hailakandi, Joint Director of Health, Labour office, Employment Exchange, Circle offices, Sub-Registrar, Fire service office.
2. e-District project has also been introduced in this district with four services,
    a. Permission for delayed birth certificate.
    b. Permission for delayed death certificate.
    c. Permission for fairs, festivals , loud speaker.
3. As regard reform measures on Revenue administration it may be stated that a good no. of reforms have been introduced which are being implemented in this district,
    a. Computerization of land records under 'Dharitri'.
    b. Constitution of village Land Management and Conservation Committee.
    c. Village Land Bank
    d. GM's Special Scheme for Rehabilitation of erosion affected families.
4. For redressal of grievances of public in general. Public Grievance Cell has been set up in this office. Grievance received from the public are disposed of on proper verification.

Conclusion

The picture reveals from the above discussion that the relevance of good governance is increasing in present days. The effective functioning of governance is the prime concern of every citizen of the country. The citizens are ready to pay the price for good services offered by the state, but what is required is a transparent, accountable and intelligible governance system absolutely free from bias and prejudices. Without good governance, a state as well as a country cannot develop economically, politically and socially. Quality of life of people of a society cannot develop without good governance. The government should continue to work on the ideals of SABKA SAATH, SABKA VIKAS AND SABKA VISHWAS which will lead to inclusive and sustainable development.

References

Bhattacherjee, M. (1996). Administration: Structure , Process and Behavior. Calcutta: World Press.

Good Governance: Needs and Challenges, *International Journal of Scientific and Engineering Research*, Volume5, Issue 5 May-2014.

Government of India. Ministry of Finance and Company Affairs. Economic Division. The Economic Survey 2003-04. New Delhi, February, 2003.

Govt. of India (2009), State and District Administration, Second Administrative Reforms Commission , 15th report.

Morris, S. (2002), The Challenges to Governance in India , India's Infrastructure Report 2002 , New Delhi

Rahim A.(2019) "Governance and Good Governance – A Conceptual Perspective", *Journal of Public Administration and Governance.*

Sheng Yap Kioe, Poverty Reduction Section UNESCAP, UN Building, Bangkok.

Tiwari, K.C. (2017) The Challenges of Good Governance in India, in the era of 21st Century. *Abhinav National Monthly Refereed Journal of Research in Commerce & Management.*

18

Quality Vs Quantity Education: An Analysis of the Implementation of FYUGP in Colleges in Assam

Kangkana Sharma

Assistant Professor,
Department of Political Science, Dhing College, Dhing
Email: skangkana1@gmail.com

Abstract

The debate between quality and quantity in education has long shaped academic discourse and policymaking in India. It is often seen that concerns of quantitative education has often been given priority in comparison to quality education as far as Indian sub-continent is concerned. The implementation of Four Year Undergraduate Programme (FYUGP) as part of National Education Policy (NEP) 2020 seeks to bridge this gap. However, the present study while analyzing the policy at length and locating it in the context of Assam argues that the implementation of FYUGP in this state presents totally a different picture.

Keywords: *Quality Education, Quantity Education, FYUGP, NEP, Higher Education*

Introduction

Categories like Quantity Education and Quality education have gained unprecedented importance in the field of learning more so in recent times. In simple sense, quality education focuses on the effectiveness of learning, ensuring that students acquire deep understanding, critical thinking, and practical skills. It is characterized by well-trained teachers, student-centered pedagogies, relevant and inclusive curricula, adequate learning resources, and a supportive learning environment. Quality education emphasizes outcomes such as literacy, numeracy, problem-solving abilities, and socio-emotional development. On the other hand, quantity education pertains to the measurable aspects of education, such as enrollment rates, number of schools, student-teacher ratios, years of schooling, and access to education. While quantity ensures broader reach and accessibility, it must be complemented by quality to ensure meaningful learning. A balanced approach integrates both dimensions—expanding educational opportunities (quantity) while maintaining high standards (quality)-to achieve equitable and sustainable development. The present paper aims to locate the

Four Year Undergraduate Programme in Assam within this context to analyse whether it aligns with the former or latter or combines both.

Background to the Study

India's education system since times immemorial had undergone significant transformations through various policies. The first initiation in this regard was done by the Kothari Commission whereby the structure of 10+2+3 was introduced. Taking a cue from the Commission, the first Educational policy was introduced in 1968 which sought to bring about egalitarianism in the educational sphere by implementing the three language formula and emphasizing compulsory education for all children upto the age of 14. Similar tone was found in the educational policy of 1986 where women, communities from Scheduled Castes and Scheduled Tribes were given prominence.

After a long journey in India's educational history, the Government of India is now transforming the education system through the implementation of the National Education Policy (NEP) 2020. As the first education policy of the 21st century, it strives to establish India as a "global knowledge superpower." The policy envisions a comprehensive overhaul of the entire education framework- including its regulation and governance- to establish a renewed system rooted in India's rich traditions and value systems.

The National Education Policy (NEP) 2020 aims to transform India's education system by shifting from rote learning to holistic, flexible, and skill-based education through a 5+3+3+4 structure, emphasizing early childhood learning, multilingualism (mother tongue till Grade 5), and vocational training from Grade 6. It promotes higher education reforms like multiple entry-exit options, a 4-year UG degree, and a single regulator (HECI), while leveraging technology and digital tools for inclusive, equitable learning. The policy also focuses on teacher training, research (via NRF), and global collaborations, striving to make India a knowledge superpower rooted in its cultural values. The Four-Year Undergraduate Programme (FYUGP), a cornerstone of NEP 2020, revolutionizes Indian higher education by introducing flexible, multidisciplinary, and research-oriented learning. It allows students to exit at different stages- earning a certificate after 1 year, a diploma after 2 years, a bachelor's degree after 3 years, or an honors/research degree after 4 years. The program encourages cross-disciplinary studies, integrates industry-relevant skills and internships, and includes a research component in the fourth year to foster innovation. With a credit-based system aligned with global standards, FYUGP aims to reduce dropouts, enhance employability, and make Indian degrees more competitive worldwide.

The NEP 2020 was implemented in the colleges of Assam from 2023 through the induction of Four Year University Graduate Programme (FYUGP). Accordingly, a total of 15 state universities started their curriculum aligning with the new framework and academic councils of all the universities had approved it.

The content of the National Education Policy (NEP) 2020 in India and the Four-Year Undergraduate Programme (FYUGP) introduced under it is structured in such a way so that it aligns itself with both quality and quantity dimensions of education. The aspects such as focus on inculcating critical thinking among students, promoting skill based education, exploring research opportunities etc.; very much incline towards the quality aspect of it. While, focusing on increase in enrolment ratio and aiming to standardize degree structures across universities for better scalability saw the policy's hunch towards quantity education.

From, the above it becomes clear that policy wise NEP 2020 and FYUGP aim to increase access (quantity) while ensuring deeper, skill-oriented learning (quality); thereby combining both. The present paper will, however, look deep into both aspects of it in the process of implementation.

Objectives

The paper focuses on the following objectives –

1. To critically examine the concepts of Quality and Quantity in Higher Education;
2. To analyse the main tenets of the Four Year Under Graduate Programme;
3. To highlight the challenges associated with the implementation of FYUGP in Assam
4. To assess the preparedness of institutions in Assam to implement the said framework.

Methodology

The paper adopts a mix of both quantitative and qualitative methods. A comprehensive review of the existing literature including policy documents (NEP 2020), government reports are done for the analysis of the subject matter. A quick survey was done amongst students (in certain colleges) about their awareness about NEP 2020 and their grasp of the current curriculum. Effort also went in to take some interviews with the faculties and policy makers associated with the drafting of this very policy.

Results and Findings

It has been almost two years since the initiation of FYUGP structure under NEP in colleges of Assam. Hence, this paper after careful analysis of the policy and its implementation, observed that the policy hasn't achieved its desired success till date. There is problem with the execution of the policy as the survey found out that most of the students are not clear about the structure of this framework. The idea of the credit system is still novel for them. Further, uncertainties loom large over the concept of internship as it will be difficult for institutions set up in rural places to follow up. Also the Skill Enhancement Course which forms an integral part of the course (as NEP focuses on employability) has remain more or less traditional with less focus on practical aspect of developing a skill or the pursuit of income generation. The NEP and the FYUGP dealt specifically with the concept of multi-disciplinary orientation but again in the real sense, it is not to be seen in most colleges in Assam. This spring from the fact many colleges in Assam are still one-streamed. Moreover, the first batch of the FYUGP course under Gauhati University always has to wait for their course structure and books in the start of every semester. Amidst this scenario, colleges themselves face difficulties in finalizing subject combination, course structures and evaluation patterns. Further, the structure of the fourth year in the Four-Year Undergraduate Programme (FYUGP) remains unclear, creating uncertainty for both students and institutions. The lack of detailed guidelines on academic content, credit requirements, and skill development in the final year raises concerns about its implementation and effectiveness.

The policy aims to expand online education and ensure its availability to everyone, even in remote regions. However, achieving this goal depends on overcoming the digital divide, which persists as a major challenge in Assam due to limited internet access in many areas. Additionally, while the policy highlights the importance of faculty development and training, the existing shortage of educators in higher education may delay institutions from building the required capacity. The most important pitfall in implementation of NEP in colleges in Assam is to do with the infrastructure which has plagued most colleges in the state. Colleges and universities will encounter major obstacles due to inadequate infrastructure, which could hinder their ability to implement education effectively. Many institutions lack reliable internet connectivity, modern classrooms (or traditional classrooms in many cases), laboratories, libraries and necessary technological resources, making it difficult to deliver quality online and offline education.

Conclusion

Any educational policy is started with a good intent but the implementation level is what that needs to be questioned. Also a particular educational policy needs to be suitable to the larger socio-cultural framework of a particular country. A framework which is successful in a developed country might not come with the same result in a developing country.

There are growing concerns about whether the Four-Year Undergraduate Programme (FYUGP) in Assam will prioritize quantity over quality in higher education. While the extended four-year framework aims to provide a more holistic and flexible learning experience, doubts persist about its actual implementation. Many fear that without adequate infrastructure, trained faculty, and clear academic standards, the programme may compromise educational quality in favor of merely increasing enrollment numbers.

In Assam, where institutions already face challenges such as poor internet connectivity, faculty shortages, and insufficient resources, rushing the FYUGP rollout could widen the gap between policy goals and ground realities. Without proper oversight and capacity-building measures, there is a risk that the additional year may become a formality rather than a meaningful enhancement of students' skills and employability.

Ensuring that the FYUGP delivers quality education—rather than just extending degree durations—will be crucial for its success in the state.

In a nutshell, it can be said that, without urgent corrective measures, this programme under NEP risks becoming a half-baked reform, widening the gap between policy promises and actual learning outcomes. However, it might be too early to presume and results will be felt in due course of time.

References

Bhushan, Sudhanshu. "Four-year Undergraduate Programme - Boon or Bane of the NEP 2020." Economic and Political Weekly Vol. 58, Issue No. 8, 25 Feb, 2023 (accessed on 23rd June, 2025, https://www.epw.in/journal/2023/8/commentary/four-year-undergraduate-programme.html

Draft. *National Education Policy 2020*. Ministry of Human Resource Development, Govt. of India (accessed on 23rd June, 2025, https://www.education.gov.in/sites/upload_files/mhrd /files/NEP_Final_English_0.pdf)

Malish. C. M. "Four-Year Undergraduate Degree as a Panacea for All?" *International Higher Education*, Issue 121, December 13, 2024 (accessed on 22nd June, 2025, https://ihe.bc.edu/pub/2q5aq3op/release/1)

Times of India Report. "Is a 4-year UG programme a bane or boon for students? Here's what Experts have to Say." Times of India, November 1, 2023 (accessed on 22nd, 2025, https://timesofindia.indiatimes.com/education/news/is-a-4-year-ug-programme-a-bane-or-boon-for-students-heres-what-experts-have-to-say/articleshow/104832031.cms)

19

Modernizing the Way We Teach: An Innovative Pedagogy in Mastering 21st Century Skills

Dr. M. Lavanya

Faculty (on Contract) in Chemistry, Department of Education,
National Institute of Technology Puducherry Karaikal (UT) of Puducherry
Email: mdlavanya2009@gmail.com

"Tell me and I forget. Teach me and I remember. Involve me and I Learn"

-Benjamin Franklin

Abstract

The 21st century is known as the Age of Digital Technology and Knowledge, where significant changes are undergoing as a result of new scientific discoveries, information technology, globalization, and the advancement of astronautics, robotics and artificial intelligence. Thus, our understanding of teaching has grown in depth and breadth in the educational process by experiencing major transformations to meet the demands and standards of an ever-changing society. Innovations and advancements are becoming constant practice to meet the transformative societal demands and expectations to achieve modernization through 21st-century teaching skills in the educational process. The purpose of the chapter is to summarize the current changes in innovative teaching methods and how to master them through practice.

Keywords: *Innovative pedagogy, 21st century skills*

Introduction

An education system strives to provide learners with the ability to understand and implement concepts in real-world situations. The rapid pace at which technology is developing makes it more difficult to meet the needs of modern society. Therefore, educational methods must be modified to satisfy the needs of society and technology. Indian institutes are transitioning from traditional to more modern teaching approaches. In the twenty-first century, educators have to figure out the most effective methods to facilitate learning. The moment has come to incorporate technical, economic, and cultural factors into all aspects of the educational system.

The twentieth century observed a significant shift in education when compared to the 21st century, where Learning has been transformed and modernized, from rote memorizing to learner-centric approaches, concept to practice, teacher-centered to student-centered, and memorization to creative thinking. It has occurred because digital media offers more flexibility than traditional media, allows for multitasking, uses intellectual ICT tools rather than relying solely on mental performance, makes textbook content easier to access with one-click internet searches, and reduces classroom interactions. As a result, knowledge acquisition transformed into knowledge creation. Thereby, the only way educators have to engage such vast audiences is with the innovative methods of instruction and pedagogy that correspond to the standards of students of new generations.

Need for Modernisation in Teaching

Historically, Teacher education has traditionally emphasized rote memory and passive learning while focusing on teaching subject-specific information and proven method of instruction. However, the challenges of the twenty-first century demand an innovative approach. The "21st-century learner" comprises digital proficiency such as critical thinking, creativity, collaboration, and communication abilities, also referred to as the "4Cs." To develop these skills among the learners, the educators need to demonstrate effectively during the time of teaching- learning process. This facilitates and modernises a fundamental change in the way that teachers teach.

In 21st century, Educators must actively integrate updated technology with an innovative pedagogy to create an evolution in the teaching process. Modernization makes sure that teaching-learning process are dynamic and interesting, which provides a more pleasurable and productive environment for the learners. In order to amplify such an environment, educators need to be possessed with the innovative tools for training. Access to data-driven insights facilitates schools strengthening student performance, thereby making education more inclusive and reaching students from underserved and remote areas. Even though remaining successful in the past, traditional chalk-and-board methods are now being supplemented with smart technologies, experiential learning, and real-time evaluation of progress to ensure that students understand concepts rather than just memorizing the facts. In order to amplify such an environment, educators need to be possessed with the innovative pedagogy to equip the way the teachers teach.

Characteristics of Modern Teaching Methods

Modern teaching has gained prominence in the contemporary teaching-learning process because of its unique characteristics. Understanding them helps you to reflect on your existing teaching methods. These are some of the key features of modern pedagogical approaches that distinguish them from their more traditional rivals.

Student-Centred Teaching

Modern teaching approaches focus mainly on the students. But in traditional teaching, the teacher is the primary source of knowledge and the decision-making process. In contrast, the primary aim of 21st-century modern pedagogical approaches is to incorporate students' learning interests and preferences. This implies that an educator must always ensure that lectures correlate with learners' abilities and interests. For example, if students are visual learners, then teaching might include more films and info graphics lessons, which may be continued by promoting active classroom involvement, soliciting regular feedback, and assessing and reflecting on the teaching methods.

Technology Integration

One distinctive feature of modern education is its collaborative nature. In this context, the use of cutting-edge instructional technology in the classroom is essential, which includes AR (Augmented Reality)/VR (Virtual Reality) sets, instructional software, interactive whiteboards, and other such technologies. The classroom can make use of an enormous variety of tools and techniques. Learners who excel in listening, for instance, may find that visualizing a video or listening to a podcast enhances their understanding. Therefore, educators must acknowledge the importance of integrating modern, innovative methods within the student community into their classroom instruction.

Critical Thinking

Modern teaching methods mainly focus on strengthening critical thinking skills and problem-solving skills through information analysis, probing, and synthesis. Instead of training the teacher trainees with some typical difficulties, Educators may teach and train them by solving the problems based on real-life scenarios and motivate them to critically investigate the facts and to discover the resolutions.

Inclusive Education

Modern teaching methods in the twenty-first century are inclusive. This implies that regardless of the learners' origins, talents, or learning styles, they ought to be able to study and develop to their maximum potential. In order to facilitate this, a modern teacher must use a variety of teaching and communication techniques that are designed to meet the requirements of various learners. The significance of innovative teaching approaches is in their capacity to establish a dynamic and egalitarian learning environment that fosters the achievement of every student.

Interdisciplinary Approach

The interdisciplinary approach is another critical component of modern teaching methods. The goal of modern teaching methods is to provide learners with a comprehensive education, which enables them to make correlations between multiple fields and concepts. This enhances their knowledge and ability to apply concepts across various subjects. For example, a science and history project may entail students investigating the technical accomplishments of historical civilizations and then building models based on their findings. This approach not only broadens students' understanding of both disciplines but also illustrates the close relationships that exist among diverse fields of study

Core Principles of Innovative Pedagogy

In the sphere of teacher education, the following primary concepts are at the forefront of enhancing and implementing innovative pedagogy.

- **Content provision to Competency building:** This shift mainly focuses on merely transmitting content knowledge into modern pedagogical approaches, which are responsible for promoting higher-order thinking skills, creativity, collaborative learning, and problem-solving ability.
- **Passive Reception to Active Construction:** Prospective educators no longer consider themselves as empty receptacles to be loaded with knowledge and information. Rather, learners take an active role in their own learning, acquiring information through research, experimentation, and critical reflection.
- **Isolated Learning to Collaborative Networks:** Recognizing the power of collective intelligence, innovative teacher education fosters collaborative learning environments, both face-to-face and online, preparing teachers to leverage the same in their future classrooms.
- **Technology as an Add-on to Seamless Integration:** Digital tools are no longer optional extras but integral components of teaching and learning, used to enhance communication, facilitate research, create engaging content, and foster digital literacy.
- **Static Curricula to Agile Adaptation:** Teacher education programs must be dynamic, continuously evolving to reflect the latest research in learning sciences, emerging technologies, and the changing needs of society

Innovative Pedagogy in Teacher Education

- **Gamification** is the practice of incorporating game design components into educational environments in order to foster learner engagement and motivation. Learning involves participation. Games that feature fascinating characters and engaging scenarios are the most efficient way to engage learners without overwhelming them with the content matter. Using games is one of the best methods to prepare learners with concept clarity before moving forward to another chapter. Thereby, learning becomes more exciting and long-lasting.
- **Spaced learning** is a more recent teaching approach that involves repeating the same lesson multiple times at varying intervals. This method provides opportunities for learners to continue their education and make connections between previously covered lessons. Before the lecture continues, the mind is refreshed by physical exercises or techniques of mindfulness; additionally,

multiple methods might be used to increase a learner's competencies. This multifaceted approach makes the learners engaged and fosters a deeper understanding of the content.

- **Collaborative Learning** makes the learners more successful by working together to solve issues, complete assignments, and make presentations for their respective lessons or topics. That is, learners can form groups, and they assist one another toward accomplishing their goals; then they become engaged, more effective participants and collaborative learners. This enables the learners to understand other people's perspectives and even meet with different people to obtain constructive feedback on their work and also share their creativity to enhance their knowledge for updating. This method plays a vital role in achieving success in both academic and professional circumstances through cultivating essential teamwork and communication skills. In addition to this, a sense of belonging and support among peers is also fostered among the learners, which is more important for social development and achieving the educational goal of success.
- **Flipped Classroom** model is the reverse model of traditional educational system where these classrooms allow the learners to watch a video tutorial, research online, or work on content shared by the teacher at home and later apply their learning in the classroom, where teachers are used to provide focused guidance for the follow up. This strategy allows the learners to interact with the subject at their own pace even during school sessions. Additionally, it optimizes the best utilization of class time by shifting teaching directly to the individual region, thereby transforming the classroom into a lively workshop and the living space into a lecture hall. This reversal fosters independent study habits besides improving understanding.
- **Cross-Learning,** in cross-cultural contexts, instruction and learning can be either formal or informal. A more informal space, such as museums, seminars, and after-school activities, is used to stir up interest and curiosity among the learners; a formal setting is utilized to instruct the subjects along with providing instructional materials that enhance understanding.
- **VAK (Visual Auditory Kinaesthetic) Teaching** Based on the multiple intelligence theory, VAK is a contemporary teaching approach. There are three types of learning: kinaesthetic (moving or feeling the data), auditory (hearing or feeling the data), and visual (seeing or hearing the data). Every learner needs their own unique method. To cater to the three main categories of learners—visual, aural, and kinaesthetic—one could utilize various mind maps and art integration for their successful learning.
- **Computational Thinking** is an effective and powerful way to think and solve problems. It entails decomposing big problems into smaller ones (decomposition), figuring out how these relate to previously solved problems (pattern recognition), putting aside irrelevant details (abstraction), figuring out and creating the steps that will be required to arrive at a solution

(algorithms), and strengthening these steps (debugging). Such computational thinking abilities may be useful in various situations, such as drafting a recipe to share a favourite meal with friends, organizing a vacation or adventure, or deploying a scientific team to address a challenging task such as a disease epidemic.

- **Project-Based Learning (PBL)** focuses mainly on real-world challenges. In this method learners are to be facilitated by innovation, collaboration, and critical thinking through developing a greater understanding of what they are learning by participating and engaging in projects. This method encourages the development about the real-life skills that are far more valuable than traditional classroom teaching. Furthermore, hands-on activities emphasize decision-making and problem-solving abilities, which are essential for the learners to accomplish their life goals in their day to day life. This is the combination of classroom instruction with global real-world applications, which equips learners to manage the multifaceted nature of the modern world
- **Digital Literacy Skills** Integrating digital literacy into the curriculum will more effectively prepare learners for facing the challenges of a digitally driven world. Learners become more capable and resilient when they acquired skills like coding, digital communication, and information technology to manage projects and assignments in the future with ease. Digital literacy also promotes safe browsing habits and critical thinking, neither of which is necessary for managing the internet's plethora of information and potential hazards. Learners who are proficient with digital tools and platforms move away from being passive consumers of learning resources to active developers of digital content.
- **Personalized Learning** provides educational experiences which are tailored to every individual learner at theirself-pace for their requirements and preferences. Educators can ensure that every learner is learning as effectively as possible by using technology to provide personalized assignments and feedback. Thus, by incorporating interests and objectives into the curriculum, education becomes more interesting and relevant for all learners through this adaptable learning environment. Personalized learning promotes diversity in the classroom by recognizing and accommodating the learners' distinct experiences and skills.

Conclusion

As educators in the 21st century, are commutable with innovative methods and techniques in their teaching-learning environment which is crucial in fostering an active participation, informative, and responsive learning environment in the classroom. By implementing all these strategies in the necessary teaching environment, teachers can ensure that their learners are not only well-prepared for their future careers but also motivated and equipped to gear up the challenges of tomorrow. The way the teacher teaches with modern innovations, by catering to varied learning styles and adapting their approach, these educators empower learners to reach their full potential, leaving a lasting impact on their academic journey and personal growth.

References

Anderson, L. W., & Krathwohl, D. R. (Eds.). (2001). *A taxonomy for learning, teaching, and assessing: A revision of Bloom's taxonomy of educational objectives*. Longman.

Bergmann, J., & Sams, A. (2012).*Flip your classroom: Reach every student in every class every day*. International Society for Technology in Education.

Deterding, S., Dixon, D., Khaled, R., & Nacke, L. (2011). From game design elements to gamefulness: Defining "gamification." In *Proceedings of the 15th International Academic MindTrek Conference: Envisioning future media environments* (pp. 9–15). ACM.https://doi.org/10.1145/2181037.2181040

Kafka, D., & Papageorgiou, T. (2025). The Pedagogy of Skills in the 21st Century: Practices for Integrating Them into the Teaching Process. Creative Education, 16, 56-70. https://doi.org/10.4236/ce.2025.161004

Kolb, D. A. (1984). *Experiential learning: Experience as the source of learning and development*. Prentice Hall.

Ministry of Education, Government of India.(2020). *National education policy 2020*. https://www.education.gov.in/nep-2020

Mynbayeva, A., Sadvakassova, Z., & Akshalova, B. (2017, December 20). Pedagogy of the twenty-first century: Innovative teaching methods. In O. Zlatkin-Troitschanskaia (Ed.), *New pedagogical challenges in the 21st century – Contributions of research in education*

Nwonwu, F. G., & Ibrahim, L. (2025, May). Innovative pedagogies for the 21st century: Transforming teaching practices through technology, inclusivity, and learner-centered approach in Nigeria. *ResearchGate*.https://www.researchgate.net/publication/articleID

Partnership for 21st Century Learning.(2019). *Framework for 21st century learning*. Battelle for Kids.http://static.battelleforkids.org/documents/p21/P21_Framework_Brief.pdf

Thomas, J. W. (2000). *A review of research on project-based learning*. Autodesk Foundation. http://www.bie.org/research/study/research_review_of_project_based_learning_2000

United Nations Educational, Scientific and Cultural Organization. (2021). *Reimagining our futures together: A new social contract for education*. UNESCO.https://unesdoc.unesco.org/ark:/48223/pf0000379707

Yakman, G. (2008). STEAM education: An overview. In *PATT-19 Proceedings: Research and practice in technology education* (pp. 335–358). https://doi.org/10.xxxxx

20

Digital Transformation in Higher Education in India

Borsha Rani Das

Research Scholar, Department of Education,
Rajiv Gandhi University, Arunachal Pradesh
Email: borsha.das@rgu.ac.in

Abstract

The integration of technology in higher education has witnessed an increase in recent years. In order to improve the teaching-learning experiences and to prepare the students for the competitive world, the higher education institutions (HEIs) are incorporating advanced technologies. However, its implementation in India is a challenge in itself. This conceptual paper discusses the technology integration in the higher education in India exploring the developments in digital revolution in the higher education, focusing on its challenges and future possibilities. The paper discusses the possible impact of digital transformation that it holds for the learners, educators and the nation.

Keywords: *Technology Integration, Digital Infrastructure, Higher Education, Teaching-Learning, Artificial Intelligence*

1. Introduction

The 21st century is also known as the digital age, has changed every aspect of our lives. Technology is leading to significant changes in the ways how we interact, we communicate with one another and how we learn. The emergence and proliferation of new technology over the last ten years have transformed various sectors. In the education sector too, technology has made its way at different levels such as from increasing administrative efficiency to improving learning among students. Technology integration in education has expanded the process of teaching and learning outside the four walls of a conventional classroom situation. The educational scenario is changing significantly in India, and the higher education institutions are leading the charge in this change. The incorporation of technology in education is operated by the need to meet the demand of the digital world and the digital natives.

Technologies such as artificial intelligence (A I), learning analytics, virtual reality (VR) and digital platforms are some of the 21st century tools that gives personalize learning experiences, improves student learning and prepares the students for tech-oriented future. Integration of Learning Management Systems (LMS) and Massive Open Online Courses (MOOCS) has redefined pedagogy, whereas digital platforms like SWAYAM (Study Webs of Active-learning for Young Aspiring Minds), NPTEL (National Programme on Technology Enhanced Learning) and Coursera provides easy access to education. Moreover, the Indian government's interest for digital education through its initiatives like Digital India and policies like National Knowledge Commission (NKC) 2005-2008 and the National Education Policy (NEP) 2020 shed light upon the growing importance of technology inclusion in education.

2. Key Forces of Digital Transformation in Higher Education

2.1 Government Programs and Initiatives- Several programs have been launched by the Indian government to foster digital education recognizing its importance to bridge educational gap. Through a range of policies, it aims to equity, access and technology ready future.

SWAYAM (Study Webs of Active Learning for Young Aspiring Minds): It is India's own MOOCs platform that offers online courses offered by various educational institutions. SWAYAM launched in 2017 seeks to bridge the digital divide and ensures equitable access to quality education (Ministry of Education). As of January 2024, 40 million plus enrolments have been made in various courses on SWAYAM and today it offers 16530+ courses in 8 Indian regional languages- Hindi, Gujarati, Marathi, Bengali, Telugu, Kannada, Malayalam and Tamil.

National Digital Library of India (NDL): The NDL is a digital repository that aims to serve as a comprehensive source of e-contents for learners at all levels. It provides access to educational resources like books, research papers, etc.

FOSSEE (Free and Open-Source Software for Education): FOSSEE promotes the use of FLOSS tools in academia and research. FOSSEE project is a part of the National Mission on Education through ICT. It aims to reduce the dependency on proprietary software in educational institutions. Scilab, Python, DWSIM, Open Modelica and Open FOAM are some of its tools.

Likewise; SWAYAM Prabha, e-yantra, virtual labs, spoken tutorial, ARPIT, National Academic Depository (NAD) are some more Indian government initiatives towards the digitalization of higher education.

2.2 **National Education Policy (NEP) 2020**- The development of technological integration in Indian higher education has gone through several crucial phases. The government introduced several policies from time to time to encourage technology integration in education. Among all, the National Education Policy (NEP) 2020 is the first policy of the 21st century that has put so much emphasis on technology integration in education recognizing its importance in today's time. The policy highlighted several initiatives for technology integration in higher education aiming towards equity, inclusivity and future-ready education system. The Academic Bank Credit (ABC), is one of those initiatives by NEP 2020, mandating digital transformation in governance processes of higher education institutions to enhance data management. As of January

2024, ABC has a strong network of 1720 registered institutions with a successful registration of 10.42 crore learners (Annual Report, Ministry of Education 2024). The policy promotes online and digital education platforms like SWAYAM (Study Webs of Active Learning for Young Aspiring Minds) and Open Educational Resources (OER) to remove digital divide. The HEIs are urged to offer virtual labs and digital libraries and to use the national learning platforms. The policy emphasizes on digital infrastructure, online digital libraries creating digital contents in regional languages, encourages short-term online courses offered through SWAYAM integrating digital skills like A.I, data analytics, etc. to address employability gap. Considering the importance of technology, it creates a National Educational Technology Forum (NETF) to create online courses in regional languages. The policy emphasized on teacher's training in digital pedagogies to equip them with skills to use LMS, AI tools and evolving technologies like VR, AR. NEP (2020) envisages internationalization through digital collaboration, global online platforms and virtual student exchange, for which the HEIs need to strengthen digital transformation skills.

3. Challenges of Digital Transformation in Higher Education

The rapid digital evolution of education has put India at a crucial point, offering both transformative opportunities and exposing persistent challenges. The country's journey towards digital transformation in its education system is both ambitious and complex. The emergence of technology has transformed traditional classrooms, introduced e-learning platforms and expanded the access to knowledge frequently. NEP 2020 along-with other digital platforms serve as a forcing agent towards creating digitally efficient citizens through education. Yet, this transformation is not uniform. The institution in urban areas possess advanced digital tools, technology supporting infrastructure facility and technologically skilled educators, whereas institution in rural areas still faces inadequate internet connectivity and infrastructure. One of the significant challenges that Indian higher education institution faces is the lack of high-quality infrastructure in rural and semi-urban areas. A significant contributing factor identified is the hindrance in funding. This shortfall includes both physical and digital infrastructure, intensifying the difficulties encountered by the State Public Universities (SPU). The lack of sufficient conference rooms suitable for digital learning and engagement poses a considerable obstacle to the successful execution of digital learning initiatives. Another significant challenge that the HEIs faces is the lack of capacity-building programs designed to improve the teacher's skills and expertise in online and digital learning approaches is a significant issue. Comprehensive training programs are needed to educate faculty with the knowledge and abilities required to employ technological tools effectively.

India is a vast country and home to over 1,600 languages spoken across the country and 22 scheduled languages recognized by the constitution. Therefore, it is necessary for digital education solutions to cater to this linguistic diversity. It is both essential and a complex task to provide inclusive digital educational resources. Platforms like SWAYAM and DIKSHA are leading the charge to democratize education by providing courses, textbooks and video lessons in several languages. Uneven access to digital resources between urban and rural learners creates the problem of digital divide.

Digital divide is a significant issue in India hindering digital education. This divide affects fair access to educational opportunities and increasing the existing inequalities. Overall, internet penetration rate of India is 65% of its population which means only 65% of India's population has access to Internet. There is a sharp division between urban and rural area's internet accessibility in India, where the internet accessibility rate is as high as 88% in Tier-1 cities. Whereas, in rural areas it stands at 37%, which clearly shows a huge gap in accessibility. This digital divide is also prevalent across the states in India with Kerala (82%) and Goa (78%) leading in internet penetration, while states like Bihar (25%) and Uttar Pradesh (30%) has the lowest internet accessibility.

Digital divide is one of the contributors to digital illiteracy. Less than one-third of people of the age group 15-29 are able to perform basic internet functioning such as sending and receiving emails, executing online transactions and do information searches. According to NSS report (2022-23) 84.8% of persons aged between 15-24, 84.2% of persons between the age group 15-29 and 59.8% of people aged 15 years and above are able to use internet. But only 26.8% of individuals aged 15-24 years, 28.5% of individual aged between 15-29 and 25.0 % of persons in the group 15 years and above in India can perform the basic online functions of sending or receiving emails, online transactions and even search for information.

Table 1: Percentage of individuals of different age groups who are able to use internet

Age Group	*Percentage of individuals able to use internet*
15-24	84.8%
15-29	84.2%
15 and above	59.8%

Table 2: Percentage of individuals of different age groups who can search internet for information, send or receive emails and perform online banking transactions.

Age Group	*Percentage of individuals performing the basic functions*
15-24	26.8%
15-29	28.5%
15 years and above	25.0%

The data above shows that there exists a huge gap between the percentage of young people being able to use internet and the individuals being able to perform the basic internet functions. This gap in basic internet skill prevails across different states of India. While the national average of students who are able to send emails, access the internet and can make online purchases is only 28.5% in the age group 15-29, there are some states that showed comparatively better performance. Among all the states, Goa leads with 65.7% of young people being able to perform; followed by Kerela with 53.4%, Tamil Nadu with 48% and Telangana with 47.2%. Conversely, states like Meghalaya (4.5%); followed by Tripura (8.2%), Chhattisgarh (11.9%) and Uttar Pradesh (16%) has the lowest percentage of people who can use these important basic digital abilities. This discrepancy shows not only the differences in the level of internet access but also in digital literacy and educational opportunities among the states.

Lack of digital literacy is another significant problem that the digital education is facing in India. It is a basic skill necessary for participating in the revolution of digital education. Lack of digital knowledge among the faculty, staff and students create hindrance in the process of digitalization. The quick adoption of digital tools in India has brought attention to these crucial gaps, that a portion of population especially in underprivileged and rural areas lacks the digital literacy needed to use these resources efficiently. To provide fair access to the advantages of digital education, this gap needs to be addressed.

Insufficiently prepared faculty and lack of training is another vital limitation in respect to adopting new technologies and including them in practice. There is a conservative mindset of many traditional-aged educators towards technology adoption in the classroom due to lower digital literacy and not being aware of new digital tools. In rural or semi-urban areas of India; the faculties struggle to use the technology in their daily pedagogy in compared to urban areas. To prepare the students for the technology-oriented world where digital skills have become an important-criteria in the contemporary job market, this gap needs to be addressed.

4. Digital Skills as Criteria in Employability Today

According to the World Economic Forum (WEF) Future of Jobs Report 2025, 92 million jobs will disappear, 170 million new jobs will emerge by 2030. It's a net gain of 78 million jobs. According to the survey, technological developments like artificial intelligence (AI) and robotics would likely be the fastest- growing job roles by 2030. The fastest growing jobs lists are Big Data Specialist, FinTech Engineers, AI and Machine Learning Specialists and Software and Applications Developers. The report clearly directing towards the trend of future job roles indicating a shift towards the AI leading the technology advancement. Healthcare, education and sustainability will experience significant expansion by 2030, while the role of administrative support, retail and customer service will slowly diminish.

The Indian graduates are unprepared for the future workforce, as the industrial sector is evolving towards artificial intelligence and automation, fresh Indian graduates are finding it difficult to keep up with it. Only 42% of Indian graduates are employable fro top technical job roles, whereas only 46.1% of Indian graduates are employable in Al and Ml roles (India's Graduate Skill Index, 2025).

A big gap between what employers need and the skills graduates have is the biggest challenge in India. Colleges in India focus more on theoretical approach than the practical skills, which is leaving the graduates unprepared for jobs. The colleges need to adopt more practical and industry-focused learning. However, in order to fill the gap between what is taught and what is needed; students, universities and its members and policymakers must act and participate in implementing the NEP 2020 in in their practices.

5. Future Prospects

Integration of cutting-edge technologies such as artificial intelligence (A.I), virtual and augmented reality (VR/AR), and blockchain has the potential to revolutionize Indian education in the future. These developments could completely transform instructional strategies, learning environments, educational administration, ensuring a more personalized, immersive and safe educational system. Digital transformation holds immense teaching-learning possibilities for the learners, educators as well as the nation.

5.1 Enhancing Learning Experiences

The inclusion of technology into higher education has brought several advantages. Artificial intelligence (AI) is transforming personalized learning by providing customized educational experiences that meets the needs and learning preferences of each individual student and learning style. While virtual reality (VR) and augmented reality (AR) technologies are taking students outside the conventional classroom and encouraging experiential and participatory learning. AR and VR creates immersive and captivating learning experiences transforming the way students engage with educational content. Furthermore, online learning platforms and Massive Open Online Courses (MOOCS) have democratized education by giving high-quality resources regardless of their location.

5.2 Equipping Educators

Digital developments not only benefit the students but also the teachers in order to deliver quality education. Teachers can concentrate more on instruction and student engagement, as the administrative duties are smoothly run by advanced learning management systems and collaborative tools. Tools like data analytics and learning analytics offers the educators insightful information about student performance, which enables the teacher to tailor their lessons and identify areas for improvement. These digital resources improve instruction's efficacy and efficiency, which eventually improves student performance.

5.3 Preparing Students for the Digital World

The world is rapidly transforming into a digital world; therefore, the higher education institutions need to prepare themselves as tech-ready institutions with technologically skilled faculty and staff members. It is crucial for the higher education institutions to prepare the students with the skills and the knowledge required for the changing world as they will be the future workforce. Digital transformation in education will foster digital literacy, critical thinking, problem-solving and teamwork abilities among students. This will prepare the students for the dynamic demands of the digital era.

6. Strategies for Effective Technology Integration

To include technology in higher education successfully, it requires a well-coordinated strategy to work on the ground level. Despite NEP 2020's insightful approach to successfully integrate technology in higher education, a number of structural obstacles are limiting its success. NEP 2020 provides an excellent roadmap towards the digital transformation in higher education. The Indian government and the HEIs should act with proper and planned measures in order to implement them in the reality.

- **Connectivity and Digital Resources:** India's internet penetration in urban and rural areas as well as among the Indian states shows a huge gap. For functional technology integration, internet access should be made available similar to electricity. HEIs in the rural and semi-urban areas must be provided the facilities like digital tools, electricity and internet access. The government should expand initiatives like BharatNet.
- **Device Accessibility:** The state governments should take the initiative of providing resources like laptops/ tablets particularly for rural, semi-urban and low-income students.
- **Faculty Capacity Building:** Skilled faculty is crucial for effective technology integration. Training should emphasize not only on ICT tools, but also on learner- centric online applications; including flipped classrooms, gamification and virtual labs and also to make them aware about this transformation.
- **Availability of Funding:** Funding to the state universities specially in rural and semi-urban areas should be taken care of by the government.
- **Collaboration with the Industries:** Partnership between HEIs and industries and EdTech companies will result in skill development programs. This will help the students to get exposure and will prepare them for the job market.

7. Conclusion

Digital evolution in Indian higher education has enormous potential for transforming the education system of the country by improving the educational opportunities bridging the digital gap and providing equity and access in education across the country. The Indian government has recognized the importance of integrating technology in education and has been trying its best in initiating programs and policies in order to foster technological inclusion in education to revolutionize the learning experiences, empower educators and preparing the students for the digital future. NEP 2020 is a landmark policy in the history of India that has given recommendations based on the changes arriving in the up-coming future. The policy addressed the employability challenges that the graduates are facing and can face in the future. The integration of technology has redefined learning experiences, making education more flexible and interactive. But country has its own disparities such as digital divide, infrastructure gaps, digital illiteracy, language barriers, etc. which is also affecting the HEI's. However, addressing the issues and ensuring fair access to digital resources is important. Strengthening faculty development training, localizing content, investing more in emerging technologies in the HEIs, collaboration of HEIs with industries, availability of funding, etc. are some areas to be prioritized. Including artificial intelligence (AI), augmented reality (AR), virtual reality (VR), flipped classroom, MOOCS in the HEIs will meet the need and learning preferences of the learners across the states promoting equity, inclusivity and accessibility. However, embracing technology in the higher education can result to a generation that is empowered and is highly competent and equipped for propelling innovation and growth in the digital era.

References

Goarty, R., & Gupta, K. P. (2025).Barriers to digital transformation in Indian higher educational institutions–a qualitative exploration of administrators' perspectives. *Education and Information Technologies*, 1-28.

Gupta, R. (2021, May). Technological Evolution of Indian Higher Education. In Gupta, Reeti (2021).Technological Evolution of Indian Higher Education. Proceedings of the NAAC Sponsored Online National Conference on 'Quality Enhancement in HEIs and Evaluation with RAF of NAAC (pp. 52-60).

Gupta, S. K., & Saranya, T. S. (2024). Navigating the digital frontier: the unique challenges and opportunities of education in India. *Pedagogy and education management review*, (4 (18)), 4-24.

Mercer-Mettl.(2025). India's Graduate Skill Index 2025. https://resources.mettl.com/wp-content/uploads/2025/02/MM_GSI_2025_Latest-1.pdf

Ministry of Education, Government of India.(2020). National Education Policy 2020. Retrieved August 01,2025, from https://www.education.gov.in/sites/upload_files/mhrd/ files/NEP_ Final_English_0.pdf

National Sample Survey Office, Government of India. (2024). Comprehensive annual Modular Survey2022-23.https://www.mospi.gov.in/sites/default/files/publication_reports/CAMS%20Report_October_N.pdf

NITI Aayog. (2025). Expanding Quality of Higher Education through States and State Public Universities.https://www.niti.gov.in/sites/default/files/2025-02/Expanding-Quality-Higher-Education-through-SPUs.pdf

PIB, Government of India. (2025). Ten Years of Digital Progress. https://www.pib.gov.in/PressNoteDetails.aspx?ModuleId=3&NoteId=154788

Varthana. (2024). The Impact of Technology on the Indian Education System

World Economic Forum.(2025). Future of Jobs Report. https://reports.weforum.org/docs/WEF_Future_of_Jobs_Report_2025.pdf